Praise f
How to Get Ri

"An extremely useful and pra ~~...~~ *...Americans—especially those who see themselves as poor—demonstrating how their money can be managed to accumulate wealth. Individuals often squander their earnings but with foresight and discipline, income can readily be diverted to savings and investments. This book should be widely read; it is a godsend for the black community."*

> —Alvin F. Poussaint, MD
> Professor of Psychiatry, Harvard Medical School, Boston, MA

"I have known Melvin Miller for twenty years, and there is not a wiser, more determined and more committed African-American entrepreneur around today. This little book can change your life. It gets right to the point, and tells it like it is. I wholeheartedly commend it to your attention."

> —Professor Glenn C. Loury
> Professor of Economics, Boston University
> Director, Institute on Race and Social Division

"Miller, a Director of the Boston Bank of Commerce, outlines the steps necessary to obtain the wealth one wants, which includes the level of desired income, budgeting, and savings."

> —Publisher's Weekly

"How to Get Rich lends its readers a real perspective on the meaning of wealth and the steps that Black America must take to gain it. A simple but effective guide to attainable wealth. You can do this!"

> —Terrie M. Williams
> Author, *The Personal Touch* and *Stay Strong: Simple Life Lessons for Teens*
> Founder, The Stay Strong Foundation

"According to Miller, a Director of the Boston Bank of Commerce, getting rich takes dicipline, determination, and a plan. He outlines the steps necessary to obtain the wealth one wants, which include determining the level of income desired, preparing a detailed budget, and counting your pennies."

> —Ann Burns, Associate Editor, *Library Journal*

How To Get Rich

When You Ain't Got Nothing

To my friend Lovell:

It is time for us to pay less attention to civil rights and begin building wealth.

Melvin B. Miller

How To Get Rich
When You Ain't Got Nothing

The African-American Guide to
Gaining and Building Wealth

By Melvin B. Miller

Amber Books
New York   Los Angeles
Phoenix

How to Get Rich When You Ain't Got Nothing
The African-American Guide to Gaining and Building Wealth

by Melvin B. Miller

Published by:
Amber Books
1334 East Chandler Boulevard, Suite 5-D67
Phoenix, AZ 85048
amberbk@aol.com
www.amberbooks.com

Tony Rose, Publisher/Editorial Director   Samuel P. Peabody, Associate Publisher
Yvonne Rose, Senior Editor   The Printed Page, Interior & Cover Design

Library of Congress Cataloging-In-Publication Data

Miller, Melvin B.
    How to get rich when you ain't got nothing : the African-American guide to gaining and building wealth / by Melvin B. Miller.
        p. cm.
    ISBN 0-9702224-8-3
    1. African-Americans--Finance, Personal. 2. Finance, Personal. 3. Investments. I.
Title: How to get rich. II. Title.

HG179 .M4598 2002
332.024'0089'96073--dc21

                                                                          2002018130

10 9 8 7 6 5 4 3 2 1

First Printing April 2002

Dedication

This book is dedicated to the men and women who are the descendants of those who were brought to America from Africa for economic exploitation. Despite adversity you have survived and grown stronger. With the passage of the Civil Rights Act of 1964 and the Voting Rights Act of 1965 you now have the legal remedies needed to secure your freedom. What remains is to develop the political clout and the wealth to assure justice and equality for our progeny.

SGMKJ

About the Author

A native of Boston, Melvin B. Miller has been actively involved in community public service for more than thirty years. In 1965, he founded the *Bay State Banner*, a weekly newspaper advocating the interests of Greater Boston's African-American community. Miller has served as the *Banner's* Publisher and Editor since its inception.

Prior to the establishment of the *Banner*, Melvin B. Miller was an Assistant U. S. Attorney for the District of Massachusetts. In 1973, the State Banking Commissioner appointed him as the Conservator of the Unity Bank and Trust Company, Boston's first minority bank.

A founding partner of Fitch, Miller & Tourse, a primarily corporate law firm. He was also Vice President and General Counsel of WHDH-TV, Channel 7 in Boston.

He is also a director of the Boston Bank of Commerce.

Melvin B. Miller is a graduate of Boston Latin School, Harvard University, and Columbia Law School.

Acknowledgment

Special thanks to my wife, Sandra,
and my daughter, Lauren, whose enthusiasm for the project
was a constant source of inspiration.
My good friend, James Venable, who has provided
the illustrations for this book
and the illustrations for *The Banner* for thirty-five years.

One of the delights in writing this book is that it will be published by Amber Books. I have known the founder and publisher of Amber Books since he was an 11-year-old living in a housing project in Roxbury, MA. Even at that young age, I could see that there was something special about him, so I decided to take him under my wing.

Perhaps it was presumptuous of me to intervene in his life, but I knew that he needed a male role model. Tony Rose is a success. He is living testimony that you can get rich even if you ain't got nothing.

I am extremely pleased that Tony Rose's skills as a book publisher will enable others to learn how you can move ahead financially when you have to start at the bottom.

Contents

Introduction

So you want to be rich. Well join the crowd. Everyone wants to be rich. It's the American way. But most people depend upon lady luck to make them rich. They hope that their lucky number will win the lottery or they will hit the jackpot at the casino. They lack a real plan to get rich. It is much better to say, "I want to get rich." That implies that you will take the necessary steps to achieve your economic goal.

The title, "How To Get Rich When You Ain't Got Nothing!" is slightly exaggerated. In order to start the process of getting rich you have to have a job, or at least the hope of a job. Unless you have a rich uncle who has agreed to set you up, then you will need your own income to get started.

Now this does not have to be a great job. It should be enough to provide for food and shelter. It is hard to think about getting rich when your stomach is grumbling and you are out in the rain and cold. But even with a very modest base income you can begin the process of getting rich.

However, the modest starting point should tell you that something else will be required to get rich—discipline and determination. Obviously you cannot get rich overnight no matter how determined you might be. Your plan for getting rich will take many years to unfold. That is why you will need discipline to stay the course.

The plan you will follow will be one that you yourself have devised. The most that I can do is to set forth the issues and the problems. You must then use this information as a guide for designing your own plan that best suits your circumstances. As you proceed and successfully carry out your plan it may be necessary to consult other sources. I have set forth in the appendix some sources which may be helpful.

You must actually write out your plan. Otherwise you are just fooling yourself. When a businessman intends to launch a new venture he prepares a business plan. This sets down precisely what he plans to do, what it will cost, what staff and equipment will be needed and when it will earn profits.

Just like a businessman you will have to lay out your plan for a period of five years. That is the only way you will be able to evaluate your progress. From time to time it might be necessary to make adjustments in your plan to accommodate unforeseen circumstances. After five years you will have to develop a new plan based upon your changed circumstances.

Remember that unless you win the lottery or receive an unexpected inheritance, you will not get rich by accident. Most folks intend to do so. And they usually follow a course of action to accomplish that goal.

It is not easy to get rich or more people would do it. It takes discipline, determination and a plan. This book can help you to develop a plan but you have to bring the discipline and determination. You cannot win without the staying power.

Remember that there will always be a consolation prize for your effort. Even if you do not become as rich as you want, you will be better off than if you did nothing.

"I guess we don't have to worry about keeping up with the Joneses no more."

–1–
How Much Is Rich?

The first question you must answer is what it means to you to be rich. This might seem like a simple question but it is very important. At some point you must establish a precise monetary goal that you are working toward. This will be rich for you. Someone else might see that number as inadequate, or too much. The concept of being rich is subjective.

America is a land of enormous wealth. Movie actors can earn $20 million for one picture. Top athletes can be paid $10 million for one season and then earn many millions more for product endorsements. The total compensation package for top business executives can exceed $50 million per year.

Such expansive incomes can support lavish lifestyles—enormous mansions, luxury automobiles, first class travel, unlimited shopping for clothes and personal items. Television and films are more than willing to make the general public aware of the "Lifestyles of the Rich and Famous."

Tragically, too many people believe that anything less than such excessive luxury is the equivalent of poverty. If your goal is Hollywood style abundance, then that is something you will probably never reach. The short and showy lives of drug dealers and rap stars could possibly influence you adversely to reach for far too much.

Just as damaging to the psyche is the American concept of poverty. Government programs to help low income families require people to confess their poverty in order to obtain benefits. When I was young such programs were unavailable. The people were reluctant to admit that they were poor. A sense of pride and optimism induced people to assert that they were only temporarily without funds. They expected their circumstance to change soon.

People seemed to understand that the concept of poverty was debilitating. It involved a crippling state of mind that made it difficult for anyone accepting that label to succeed. Most of the people who would be considered poor in the neighborhood of my youth eventually fought their way up to middle class status.

If you think of yourself as poor, give up that notion. It usually means that one lacks the resources to live in a style to which he would like to become accustomed. Of course there are some families which lack the necessary income to sustain even a modest standard of living. Nonetheless, poverty is often a state of mind.

In 1972, while running for public office, I visited with some families in public housing. One woman's apartment was roomy and well furnished. A large color television console occupied a prominent position in the living room. This was before color TV had fully penetrated the market. In my conversation with the women, they made it clear that they considered themselves poor. When they found out that I did not have a color TV they were sympathetic, as though I had fallen on hard times.

The opposite of being rich is not to be poor. Many people who just get by cannot be said to be poor, but neither are they rich. If you have a "poor" state of mind, you must get rid of it if you want to get rich. To be poor implies a sense of hopelessness. You must believe that you have the capacity to become rich.

As a group, African-Americans are by no means poor. The total annual income of all African-Americans in America is about $500 billion. If black America were a separate country it would have the 11th highest gross national product (GNP) of all nations in the world. The nations with a higher GNP would include: United States, Japan, Germany, France, United Kingdom, Italy, China, Brazil, Canada and Spain. The African--American GNP is still greater than India, Korea, Netherlands, Australia, Mexico, Russia, Argentina, Switzerland, Belgium, Sweden and Austria. By comparison with other nations, then, African-Americans are rich. The problem is that African-Americans living in the United States are part of an incredibly wealthy nation. Americans, the wealthiest nation in the world, set a standard of affluence which is incredibly high.

For example, the public housing apartment I visited would be considered luxury housing in India. Some of the apartments sought after by middle class professionals in India would be considered to be unsatisfactory to many families on welfare in the United States.

Of course you live in the United States so that is the standard that we will adopt. But it is good to have a broader view of your economic status. Your present condition and your opportunities should appear to be much more promising by comparison to world standards.

When you think of getting rich you must first think of the level of income you desire. This is your plan and you must set your own objectives. Be optimistic, but also be realistic. An income goal that can never be reached will only lead to frustration.

Remember that whatever income you choose you will have to earn. It might require working two jobs, but that is not unusual for someone just starting the process of getting rich. Such hard work is not really what we think of for someone who is already rich. Their income comes from a trust fund or from dividends from investments.

That brings us to what is the real foundation of wealth for a rich person—assets. The wonderful thing about assets is that they work for you while you play. If you had $2,000,000 invested in securities paying 5%, you would earn $100,000 per year for doing no more than waking up and smelling the flowers.

Clearly assets are better than income earned from a salary. You have to work hard to earn your salary. The whole objective of the plan you are in the process of developing is to increase the value of your assets. An individual's net worth determines whether you are really rich. The net worth is the value of your assets minus all liabilities. Your assets will include your cash, investments and real estate. The total of the outstanding balance of your mortgage, auto loan, credit card debt and any other loans determines the amount of your liabilities.

In addition to providing income, wealth influences where you can live, whether you can afford private school for your children, whether it is feasible to start a business, and when and whether you can afford to retire.

While the gap between the income of African-Americans and European-Americans is narrowing, there is an enormous racial gap in wealth. The average wealth of African-American families in 1999 was $37,929, but for European-American families it was $248,961. Projections indicate that this gap is unlikely to close. When your get rich plan succeeds, you will have overcome great odds.

—2—

The Basic Plan

The first step of your plan is to prepare a detailed budget. This is not simply listing all of the bills you owe. That would be much too easy. It is necessary to go over every current expenditure to determine how you can spend less for every item.

This is the acid test. You must face the conflict between consumption and investment. Everyone is bombarded with advertising that enflames your desire for everything in the world. But how much of that stuff do you really need? Money saved by not submitting to the advertisement can be invested to make you rich.

It will require enormous discipline to resist the many temptations. Visions of future financial security might be a motivating spark. When my father got his paycheck, he always said the first thing he did was pay himself. He put aside the money that he planned to save first. Then he paid the household bills.

He was diligent about saving money for the college education of his six children. Dad decided that since there was not much he could do to increase his income substantially, he had to devise ways to spend less on household expenses while still maintaining a comfortable life style.

He knew where to shop for the best bargains. We bought fruit and vegetables from the street vendors on Saturday afternoon when the prices had dropped. He bought his children quality clothes at discount prices. Every fall we would go to the shoe factories to buy shoes for school. They were the same shoes that sold for twice as much in the retail stores.

Through his careful handling of money my father provided a comfortable life for his family. He always owned a car and we lived in a house which he owned. All of his children who chose to go to college had his financial backing. When he died at the age of 92 he left an estate of almost one million dollars. That is not bad for a African-American man born in the 19th century who did not have the opportunity to finish high school. And he accomplished this on the salary of a U.S. Post Office employee.

Now you can see why I refused to say that I was poor when I was running for public office. That would have been pro-foundly disrespectful of my father's sacrifice. Because of my father's discipline and determination I had everything I needed as a child.

When I was still a young boy my father enlisted me as his assistant on his weekend shopping excursions. He taught me how to recognize quality in clothing and other merchandise, and he made me mindful of prices when shopping for groceries. These are skills which I still put to good use.

When I started the *Bay State Banner*, at the time Boston's only African-American weekly newspaper, it was clear that the meager capital would not provide a salary for me. As is often the case when establishing a new business the amount of investment capital is inadequate. I had saved a little money from my salary as an Assistant U.S. Attorney, but that was clearly not enough. The only solution was to undertake a program of severe austerity.

I knew I had to cut my budget to the bone. At the time I smoked and was a social drinker. Neither contributed to my nutritional requirements so both were eliminated. Soda and many processed food items were cut from the budget. Since I knew I would be working terribly long hours there was not need for an entertainment budget. Getting a few extra hours of sleep was the most satisfying way to spend any free time. I also moved out of my roomy apartment and took a room with a friendly family.

This was a very Spartan budget, but I knew I would not have to do it forever. Either the Banner would do well and I could go on payroll or it would tank and I would get a good paying job. However, the sacrifice was necessary for some time.

I can still remember that period of my life, 35 years ago. I owned nothing except some books and my clothes. It was a very liberating sensation. There was nothing to take care of except for the Banner. The very simple diet I lived on was undoubtedly healthier than what I had been eating. The only difficulty was adjusting to the lack of privacy that is imposed upon a roomer.

Such extreme austerity is not an option for most people, especially if they have a family. I was single at the time. Nonetheless, the only way you can hope to get rich is to save and invest substantial amounts of your income. Be careful about every expenditure. Remember that money spent on consumption is money that cannot be invested to make you rich.

Your biggest enemy will be the tendency to ignore the significance of small expenditures. How many times have you said, "Oh well, it's just another dollar." But those dollars add up. If you could save $10 per week on your family's food bill, that would give you $43 per month to invest. If you did that for 30 years, the same period of time it takes to retire a home mortgage, with a compound annual rate of return of 10% you would have $98,011.

Now that is not enough money to make you rich, but it does illustrate how an insignificant amount of money prudently invested instead of spent on something non-essential can grow over time. Just think what the result might be if you could save 10 times the $43 a month. Now you would have almost a million dollars and could be considered to be rich.

One place to save is on transportation. It costs only $134 a month to lease a Ford Focus, compared with $399 for a Mercedes E320 or a Lexus IS300. And the beloved Beamer

525I goes for $499 a month. Just think how much you could save for investment if your ego did not require you to show up in style behind the wheel of a luxury car. I have a friend who is worth several hundred million dollars, and he drives an old Chevy.

Let's face it, if you want to be rich you have to organize your spending patterns around maximizing investments rather than maximizing consumption. There will be no keeping up with the Joneses unless the Jones family are compulsive savers and investors.

If you are unwilling to cut your budget and save you will never get rich. You can only hope that Lady Luck will have the lottery pick your number. Save your energy. There is no need to read further. This book is not for you.

"You better stop your dreaming and come on down to earth."

—3—
The Numbers Game

I hate to count pennies. You probably hate it too. But unless your income is at such a substantial level that minor purchases need not be noted, you will have to develop a penny counting skill if you want to get rich. Are you going to pay yourself or pay the man?

It has always amazed me that we can work so hard and then be so careless about how we spend our hard earned paycheck. There is a gas station in my neighborhood that charges about 50 cents more a gallon than at other stations selling brand name gasoline. Nevertheless there are always cars waiting at the pump.

If you want to develop a plan and get rich you will have to monitor every purchase you make for a period of three months. It will not be enough to list $90 for groceries. You will have to keep the sales slips and note every item purchased. If this sounds tedious, it is no more demanding than what you do to count calories to lose weight.

There are two things you will be trying to determine from this process. First, how much money did you spend on junk food—processed items that taste good but have little nutritional value. Secondly, you will want to determine whether the store where you shop offers the best prices for the items you really need.

Then you want to determine how much money you spend on entertainment. That category would include sports games, nightclubs, movies, records and cds, health club dues, hobbies, restaurants, parties and other social events. Now here comes the pain. Maybe you can do without those extra potato chips and six-pack of beer. Fine. You have to decide what you are willing to sacrifice to get rich.

Let's look at your clothes budget. Are you planning to make some major purchases from the fall collection at that fancy boutique? This category should not be a serious problem unless you are a slave to designer labels. Do you feel compelled to be in step with every new fad? It's your call.

How much does your car cost you? What percentage of your after tax income is that? Are you spending too much? Are you paying the best price for gas? Those folks who pay 50 cents a gallon more than they have to could save at least $20 a month.

I will not get into the question of reducing housing costs because the possibilities for doing this vary so greatly from city to city. Just give the issue some thought.

We develop patterns of living which soon become habits. We humans like habits because we can function on automatic drive. It is not necessary to think of all the many things to be done. It becomes a reflex action. Watch people shopping in the grocery store. They make the same rounds week after week. There's not much to think about. What you have to do is change your habits so that you are able to maximize your investments.

There are some habits that are both expensive and harmful. At today's prices, a person with a pack a day cigarette habit spends about $100 a month on smoking. Over a period of 25 years he will have spent $30,000, if he lives that long. If that money was invested in a dynamic growth fund for that period, it could probably earn an average annual compound rate of return of 12%. That would come to $187,885.

Undoubtedly there are those who smoke while insisting that they cannot afford to save and invest. What they are really saying is that smoking gives them greater satisfaction than being rich, so they are unwilling or unable to make the necessary sacrifices to get rich. Instead the tobacco industry is getting rich off them. Those who spend an excessive amount of money on alcoholic beverages are in the same boat. Unfortunately those who have become addicted to drugs have completely lost control of their lives.

Another item that can ruin your budget is excessive debt. It is hard to resist using those credit cards which are so easily acquired. Every week notices arrive in the mail that you have been approved for a new card. The sales pitch often has flattering comments about your financial probity. The temptation to respond is great.

The greatest inducement is a very low initial interest rate. It seems like free money. But when you do not repay the loan during the honeymoon period the interest rate skyrockets. Your first job is to pay off all of those high interest loans and resist starting the process all over again.

Now we have to get down to the hard work—running the numbers. On the following page is a form for your current budget. In order to fill out the annual income figures, multiply the numbers on your paycheck by 52 if you get paid every week. Multiply by 26 if you get paid every other week. You pay most of your bills monthly. So you multiply the amount by 12. For your food bills, keep receipts for one month and then add them up to get the total.

Following the budget form is the worksheet. That is for analyzing your food budget. If you have no interest in trying to save money on food, simply ignore it. Just use the total figure on your budget form.

Make photocopies of all the forms you plan to use. An extra copy of the budget form should be used to write out your revised budget as part of your get rich plan.

BUDGET

	Income	Deductions
Payroll I		
Federal Taxes		
State Taxes		
Social Security		
Medicare		
401 (K)		
Total		
Payroll II		
Federal Taxes		
State Taxes		
Social Security		
Medicare		
401 (K)		
Total Payroll		
Fees—Estimated Taxes		
Interest—Estimated		
Dividends—Estimated Taxes		
Expenditures		

Mortgage
    Principal
    Interest
    Home Owners Insurance		

Rent		

Utilities
    Electricity
    Gas or oil
    Telephone		

Credit Cards
    Card 1
    Card 2
    Card 3		

	Income	Deductions
Life Insurance		
Health Insurance		

Automobile Payment
    Car #1
    Car #2		

Automobile Insurance
    Car #1
    Car #2		

Auto Repairs		
Gasoline		
Food		
Clothes		

Entertainment
    Movies
    Clubs
    Vacations		

Gifts		
Furniture		
Household Items		

FOOD BUDGET

ITEM	MONTH 1	MONTH 2	MONTH 3
Meats			
Fish			
Milk			
Cheese			
Butter			
Fresh Vegetables			
Fresh Fruit			
Cereal			
Juices			
Soft Drinks			
Coffee-Tea			
Ice Cream			
Cookies			
Canned Goods			
Frozen Goods			
Condiments			
Toiletries			
Snack Foods			

–4–
They See You Coming

There is a history of economic abuse of African-Americans in America. That is what slavery was all about. But the economic exploitation of African-Americans did not end when slavery was over. We know from the Juneteenth celebration that plantation owners in Texas simply did not tell their slaves for two years that slavery had been outlawed. Back then in the 19th century there were no massive communications media to get the word out, so the slave owners just decided to keep silent.

A notorious economic crime that launched the modern civil rights movement was the requirement that African-Americans ride in the back of the bus. That was viewed as a social indignity because the rule discriminated against African-Americans, but it was more than that. This policy was also an economic abuse because African-Americans were obligated to pay full fare but were afforded second class privileges.

Once during the days of American apartheid I bought a bus ticket in Tulsa, Oklahoma to travel to Dallas. The ticket agent directed me to the colored waiting room, which was the size of a large closet fitted with backless wooden benches. The room was painted some years ago in institutional beige which was now peeling. A bare bulb hanging from a wire cast hardly enough light to read.

By contrast, the other waiting room was well lit, roomy and fitted with upholstered sofas and chairs for the comfort of the customers. Little tables were provided to make it easier to handle food from the snack bar. We could come out of our holding pen to buy food at the place provided at the end of the snack bar, but we had to return immediately to the pen once the order was filled.

I objected to the ticket agent that while the accommodations were indeed separate they were by no means equal so I expected a reduction in the price of my ticket. I told him that I did not at all object to sitting in the company of my brothers and sisters, but I did not expect to pay a full, but unequal fare to do so.

When he refused to give me a discount I went and sat in the first class lounge since that is the price I had paid. He left to get the police he said. Fortunately for me, the bus came before he returned, so I left.

The moral of this story is that some people have developed a tradition of overcharging us, and we have developed a tradition of paying the price to avoid trouble. The man says an item costs a certain price and we are often reluctant to challenge it. This tradition survives because haggling over price is not customary in the United States as in the Middle East , Africa or Southern Europe.

If you do not comparison shop for major purchases, you will be spending money needlessly and reducing your resources available for investment. When it is time to buy a house, check with the mortgage finance companies and the banks in your area to find out which one offers the lowest rate of interest. But don't stop there. Also find out the application fees and other filing and attorney's fees each institution charges. Sometimes a low interest rate does not tell the whole story.

The purchase of your own home will be a major event in your family's life. But be prepared for the realities of home owner-ship. At some point you will need a plumber, an electrician, a painter or a carpenter. Be prepared. Find the contractors you will need in advance so that you will not make a bad decision when confronted with an emergency.

Be aware of one of America's persistent scams, the home improve-ment contractor. If you need some major work done on the house, never sign a contract with a salesman just because he seems so very nice. His attitude will probably change once you sign on the dotted line.

Do some research. Find a number of reputable contractors who are proficient and experienced in the work you need. Have each of them submit a detailed bid. You will ordinarily need three bids to get the job financed by your bank. If it is a major job, have a lawyer review the contract before you sign.

The home improvement scam artist rips you off two ways. First he charges too much for the work he does. Sometimes he will even persuade you to fix something that isn't even broken. And then he charges an outrageous interest rate when he arranges for the financing of the job. The customer is lulled to sleep because the scam artist will take care of everything.

Buying A Car

Another major purchase is a car. There are three ways to be ripped off when buying a car. The first is that the dealer gives you too little for your used car. The second is that he charges you too much for the car you want to buy. And the third is that he charges too high a rate of interest for the financing.

A recent report indicates that African-Americans paid more for Nissan cars than others with an equal credit profile. More money was squeezed from African-Americans by charging more for interest to finance the purchase. This practice is quite common in the auto industry.

The extra interest can be quite substantial. The report indicates that the average finance costs paid by African-Americans was $800 greater than what European-Americans paid. One study indicates that since 1990, African-American Nissan customers paid roughly $840 million in extra interest.

This is the way it works. The banks or finance companies set interest rates for customers with various credit profiles. If the dealer can induce the customer to pay more than what the bank requires, the difference is called the dealer markup. The dealer splits this extra interest with the financing institution, but the dealer keeps the larger share.

Your objective must be to get the dealer's preferential rate, the lowest rate for a customer in your financial and credit category. Shop around. Once you know what make and model you want, go to competing dealers. See who offers you the best deal.

Before you go you should know what your present car is worth if you plan to trade it in. You can get the Kelly Blue Book value on the internet. Go to www.kbb.com and look up your model and year. The Blue Book price is the prevailing price in the market. Consider the closest price to that on your trade in as money saved.

You should also learn the standard price for the car you want to buy. Go to the internet again and look up www.edmunds.com and www.autotrader.com. These sites will tell you the price and all of the operating information about the car you want. The more knowledgeable you are when you go to the auto dealer the less likely the salesman is to believe he can take advantage of you.

Don't be afraid to say, "NO!" Get up and walk out if the dealer refuses to give you the deal you want. There are other agencies. Sometimes, when the dealer sees that you won't go for his scam he might call you at home a week later and tell you that he did some homework and found just the deal you want.

Second Mortgages

Two circumstances can make you eligible for a second mortgage. Either you have substantially paid down your first mortgage or the value of your real estate has increased substantially. If you bought a house for $150,000 and it is now worth

$250,000, you have an extra $100,000 in value based upon the price. But if you have also paid off $60,000 of the principal of the first mortgage you then have $160,000 in equity.

Many banks and finance companies have been advertising equity loans. They are good business for the banks because the interest rate is substantially higher than the first mortgage rate. Nonetheless, these loans are often attractive to customers who have become over-committed on credit card loans.

Before you do anything, check the rate of interest on your mortgage. If the present interest rate is much lower, it is time to refinance your mortgage. If you have a $130,000 mortgage for 30 years at 8%, you will pay $953.89 per month for debt service. The same mortgage at 6.5% will cost $821.66. That is a saving of $132.20.

Since you have only $70,000 left to pay off on the original mortgage and you need another $30,000 to pay off sundry debts, in a competitive environment your bank might be willing to rewrite the mortgage and give you $30,000 in cash. You will have to do the math to determine what is the best deal.

The rate the bank asks might be more than the 6.5% you could get on a straight re-write. It would undoubtedly be better than the double-digit rate banks usually charge on seconds. At any rate, the experience should teach you to avoid credit card debt.

The man is looking for a chump. Don't oblige him.

–5–
Income

Once you begin implementing your "get rich" plan faithfully, a strange change in your outlook will occur. You will begin seeing additional income as an opportunity for investment rather than a means to buy more consumer goods. You will become free of the consumption madness which besets most Americans.

This can be a time of conflict for married couples, especially when both spouses work. It is crucial for husband and wife to have extended discussions on the plan so that both are in agreement. Beware that disagreements about money are one of the primary reasons families can disintegrate. It is important for both spouses to be in accord with the plan.

The source of contention will be how much to save. No matter how austere the budget, it will become obvious that the amount to be saved will be constrained by the size of the income. It is highly unlikely, for example, that a family of four with an after tax income of $600 per week could save half.

In a business, revenue comes from sales. For working people revenue comes from their paycheck, no matter how large or small that may be. Businesses develop advertising campaigns and other strategies to increase sales. Working people have to get another job or find a more lucrative line of work. In an extreme case they may even have move to a place where good jobs are available when opportunities dry up where they live.

Just as business executives plan carefully when about to begin a campaign to generate sales revenue, you should do the same when planning to increase income. It makes little sense to prepare for a field which is dying out. This is especially important now because of the shifts occurring in the American economy.

The first step is to determine how your income stacks up with incomes of other taxpayers. If you are fortunate enough to be one of the households with the top 1% of after tax income, you are in the fastest growing segment. Incomes in this category increased from $263,700 in 1979 to $677,900 in 1997.

During this same period, after tax incomes for the lowest earning one-fifth fell from $10,900 after taxes to $10,800. The middle fifth group went from $43,880 on average to $47,200. This is a growth of 8 percent for middle-income families compared to 157 percent for the wealthiest 1 percent.

As you might expect, the income of African-American families falls in the lower ranges. In 1995 the median income of households was $45,018 compared with only $25,970 for

African-Americans. The median statistic tells you that the same number of households earned more than $25,970 as less than that income.

The racial income disparity is more clearly understood by noting the differences in different income ranges. Only 22.6% of European-American households earn less than $25,000 compared to 48.5% of African-Americans. On the other hand only 21.3% of African-American households earn more than $50,000 compared to 44.0% of European-Americans. The percentages in the range from $25,000 to $35,000 are roughly equivalent.

Racial discrimination is responsible for some of this disparity. European-American families are more than twice as likely as African-Americans to earn more than $50,000 per year. And African-Americans are more than twice as likely as European-Americans to earn less than $25,000. However, the chances of falling in the mid-range, $25,000 to $35,000, are just about even. This indicates that there are also other factors at work.

Numerous studies have established that the difference is education. Slaves understood this, but it seems that their wisdom has been lost. The fervor for education among African-Americans is not now what it once was. Over the years African-Americans have closed the gap with European-Americans over the percentage of high school graduates. However, there is some question about the quality of the high school education received by some African-Americans.

Many high school graduates have still not attained the level of literacy needed to function effectively in the new economy. It is not enough to write your name and read simple statements. The National Adult Literary Survey (NALS) has established five levels of literacy. According to the NALS, level 3 is the minimum necessary to perform at the level required today. This would enable one to prepare a synopsis from a news article or plan travel arrangements from a flight plan.

The level of literacy skills will have an impact on salary. Those high school graduates who have attained only the basic NALS level 1 earn on average only $350 per week, while those at level 3 earn an average of $425 per week. On an annual basis that is the difference between $16,900 and $22,100.

The number of years of formal education has a major impact on the income you can receive. National data show that male college graduates aged 25-34 earned 52 percent more than high school graduates.

The difference was even greater for women. Women college graduates earned 91 percent more than high school graduates. Even those with some college earned 28 percent more. Those with 2-year associate degrees can expect about half the premium of college graduates 26 percent for males and 45 percent for females.

Now the situation should be clear. You must have a good understanding of the economic ground rules as you make plans to increase your income. In brief, the economy is changing to a technology and information base. The unskilled factory and labor jobs so important 20 years ago are disappearing. More than a high school diploma is now needed to land a job that pays well. Higher education and a high rate of literacy are also essential.

There is a good chance that a well-qualified African-American can land a job in the $25,000 to $35,000 range. However, competition for jobs paying $50,000 or more is pretty fierce. My father always said that you have to be better prepared and more qualified to have any hope of overcoming racial discrimination in employment.

Don't be dismayed if you never finished high school. Research indicates that those with a GED outperform high school graduates who choose not to opt for higher educations. That makes sense if you think about it. Too many people are awarded a high school diploma for doing little more than showing up. You have to pass some examinations to demonstrate your competence to be awarded a GED, and you have to be motivated to even try.

Whether you are seeking a GED, special job training programs, a certificate or an associate degree from a community college, your State Board of Education will have the information you need. Appendix A lists the addresses and telephone numbers for that agency in every state. State employment agencies also provide job counseling and may sometimes offer special training. The address and phone number of your state employment agency is in Appendix B.

–6–
Mr. and Mrs. Incorporated

When there is a wedding, everyone's attention is on the joining of the bride and groom in an intimate relationship. Few are aware that a new economic unit has been formed.

That is not the case with the very rich. Before the wedding both parties will more than likely have signed pre-nuptial agreements to determine in advance the division of property in the event of a divorce. If the bride and groom are from prominent families, there is often much speculation about the economic significance of the merger.

The formation of a family is one of the most dynamic forces in the economy. The African-American median household income in 1998 was $25,351, substantially less than the $40,912 income level for European-Americans. However, the income level increases substantially for African-American married couples to $47,382. This is almost $7,000 greater than the median for all European-American households and is only $7,463 less than the median income for European-American married couples ($54,845).

Unfortunately, married couples tend to focus almost exclusively on the quality of their interpersonal relationships. Because of the racial hostility in the outside world, African-American spouses expect quite a bit from one another. Sometimes this is a burden that neither can satisfactorily shoulder.

For decades before it was fashionable for European-American, middle class wives to work outside of the house, African-American housewives in great numbers held outside jobs. They were middle class—they certainly had middle class values. But because of discrimination their husbands could not find jobs that paid them an appropriate salary. So the wives went to work.

The racial discrimination so constant in the workplace is very irritating. It takes extraordinary control not to bring this anger home. Unfortunately, our loved ones often have to bear the brunt of this anger. The relationship is put under even more stress because television and other media give a distorted view of what to expect.

As a child I was aware of the strain in my parents' relationship. It was clear to me even then that money was one of the sources of the conflict. My mother was more carefree about money so my frugal father did not trust her to do the shopping. Very often disputes over money cause marriages to fail.

For many African-Americans a failed marriage can result in economic disaster. The median income for African-American men in 1998 was $19,321 and the median income for African-American women was $13,137. When a marriage dissolves, expenses increase, especially if there are children. The financial problems can become so onerous that the possibility of getting rich is seriously compromised.

As an adult I asked my father how he endured discrimination on the job and stress and home. His response was very instructive. He said that he had six children so he just focused on the next generation. Reflecting on his experience in World War I he said, "sometimes it was the job of the first wave out of the trenches to lay across the barbed wire so that those who followed could move forward more easily."

My father taught me the importance of having concern for the welfare of future generations. This is actually an instinctive impulse. That is how the species survives. Unfortunately some African-Americans have lost sight of this drive because of the difficulty of personal survival. As recently as 1970 the average age of mortality for the African-American male was only 60 years.

Times are a bit easier now. As of 1998 the average age of mortality for African-American males had climbed to 67.6 years, 7.2 years less than the African-American woman. Now the African-American male lives long enough to collect social security, and if he is married his widow can collect.

Social conditions now support the concept of parents sacrificing to ease the way for their children. Once you begin the process of getting rich it almost happens naturally. You are forced to plan for the future because it is impossible to get rich overnight. The future always involves the welfare of your children as adults.

So many of our forefathers had to hurl themselves across the barbed wire to provide an easier path for us. For this reason the idea of "giving back" to the community is a generally accepted idea. The first step is to plan for your family, or else how can we give to the community?

"I never thought I'd be working a second job just to get more money to invest."

–7–
Finding the Job

After completing your education you are ready to find that ideal job. The economy of your region will determine what kinds of jobs are available in the private sector. Also do not overlook the job opportunities in state and federal government.

Information on federal jobs is available at regional employment offices. The address and phone number of the employment information center closest to you are in Appendix C. They should be able to tell you the jobs that are available for candidates with your qualifications and what the pay scale is. State employment centers list the government jobs available in each state. The agency for your state is shown in Appendix D.

I know that you are flushed with pride over your academic achievements and your newly acquired skills. But remember this, the tragedy of America is that for many decades competent, qualified African-Americans were denied employ-ment at their appropriate level. Harvard College graduates worked as hospital orderlies and redcaps. The issue has not been qualifications.

You must know that the attitude which denied employment to qualified African-Americans in the past is not dead. You have a better chance today but it is still no slam dunk. You will still lose if you make a bad impression in the interview.

There is a strange opinion among some African-Americans that they have the right to dress any way they want or wear any extreme hairstyles and the rest of the world is obligated to accept it. Let me assure you that they won't. Interviewers are reluctant to take a chance on someone who appears to be out of step with their corporate culture. They will simply find an acceptable way to say no.

Several years ago there was a brilliant African-American stu-dent at Harvard Law School. In his first job interview he showed up in his most stylish chartreuse suit. The interviewer was very cordial but clearly not interested. At the end of the interview he said, "I am sorry but our firm does not handle cli-ents in the entertainment industry."

The student got the message. He showed up for later interviews in the drab ivy league uniform with a button down shirt. Need-less to say those later interviews were much more successful.

Just the reverse situation was true during the recent dot com craze. Most of those companies were run by very young people who advocated very casual attire at work.

The point is that what you wear is a uniform. Be out of uniform at your own peril. Professional organizations will usually not tolerate dreadlocks, cornrows, or twisted locks among their professional staff. They will consider women in come hither attire to be too provocative and dangerous, an invitation for a sexual harassment suit.

I know that the hip-hop style is in vogue, but it has unfortunately also been adopted by the gang bangers. You are undoubtedly an upstanding member of society, but strangers don't know that. It would be unwise to dress and behave in a way that triggers the interviewer's fears.

If a resume is required for the job, it pays to have one professionally done. An employer expects you to put your best foot forward when applying for a job. If your resume is sloppy, he will believe that is the best that he can expect from you.

There is nothing more unsettling and nerve-wracking than to apply for a job. It is natural to be nervous but you must show that you are confident. Practice with a friend beforehand so that your responses to questions are clear and articulate. Many communities have services that will help you prepare.

I believe that if you are a person who is determined to exercise the necessary discipline to get rich you will make an excellent employee. Good luck!

–8–
Entrepreneur

There are those who don't want a job. They want to work for themselves. They want to be in business. The story of the ambitious businessman who starts with nothing and builds an industrial empire is a common American fable. Of course it happens, but the rate of failure for new businesses is substantial. You have to be certain that you have the necessary tolerance for risk if you choose to tread this path.

There are essentially three ways to go into business. First, you can buy an existing business. Secondly, you can buy a national franchise, or third, you can start from scratch. There are advantages and disadvantages to each approach.

If you buy an existing business you will have the advantage of being able to review the financial statements for a period of time and become aware of the company's record of profitability. Usually the price will be based upon some factor times earnings. If the factor is 10 and the annual profit is $1,000,000, the sales price will be $10,000,000.

The risk is that there might be circumstances unknown to the buyer which will greatly reduce future profits. In that case the buyer will have paid too much for the company.

Buying a going concern, nonetheless, reduces the number of risk factors the entrepreneur faces by starting from scratch. A middle position is to buy a franchise. The franchiser will have done extensive national advertising to establish the brand. He will also have worked out the procedures for running the business. The entrepreneur must simply determine whether there is an adequate market for his product where he plans to establish the business.

If the franchise approach appeals to you, a list of franchise directories is at Appendix E. Be aware that the greater certainty of success offered by a franchise comes at a price. The franchiser will be entitled to a share of your profits, from 3% to 10% of gross income. You must also be sure that the franchiser really provides all that he promises. Never enter into such an agreement without the help of a good lawyer.

Starting from scratch is clearly the riskiest approach. But you need not be without sound advice and professional resources if you decide to leap in. The Federal Small Business Administration has numerous programs to assist you. If you plan to go into business, the first thing you should do is contact your local SBA office. See Appendix F to find the closest office to you.

Probably the most valuable SBA programs provide loan guarantees. As a new businessman, you have not yet developed a favorable track record. Like most entrepreneurs, your personal financial resources will undoubtedly not provide enough capital. Because you also lack sufficient collateral a bank will normally be unwilling to extend a loan.

In comes the SBA. They will guarantee repayment of 70% of the value of the bank loan. Such loans cannot exceed $750,000 and can carry an interest rate of no more than 2.75 percent over the prime rate. The prime rate is the rate of interest that the bank charges its most secure customers. These loans can mature in up to 10 years for working capital and 25 years for fixed assets. There are various forms of the loan programs for you to investigate.

One of the most difficult problems for small construction companies is to obtain a surety bond. Their customers will require that all of the work covered by the contract will be completed in a workman like manner at the agreed contract price. Understandably, surety companies are reluctant to take that risk with a new company. The SBA will guarantee surety bonds up to $1.25 million.

Another invaluable SBA program is called SCORE, Service Corps Of Retire Executives. Business executives with experience in your industry will serve as consultants to you at little or no cost. When you are starting out in a new business there is much to learn. Your SCORE associate will speed you along the learning curve.

Most states also have programs to stimulate the development of businesses. These will differ in scope from state to state. Your SBA office will certainly know what they are and will refer you to them.

Whether you want to buy a business, buy a franchise, or start a business from the ground up, the SBA and the state business development programs will be helpful. But in any case you will be expected to contribute some equity. They will want it to be painful for you to walk away from the business if things go bad. So if you want to go into business be prepared to go into hock and to work endless hours.

As an African-American you are qualified to receive the benefits of the Minority Business Development Centers which have been established by the U.S. Department of Commerce to assist with the start–up and expansion of minority owned firms. The services provided include business assistance in bonding, mergers and acquisitions, financing procurement, franchising and international trade.

These centers are financed by the U.S. Government but are owned and operated by private firms, state and local governments and educational institutions. A list of the centers in the various states is found in Appendix G. Or you can contact National Headquarters of Minority Business Development Agency, U. S. Department of Commerce, Room 5099, Washington, D.C. 20230, telephone 202/482-3007.

—9—

Saga of the Entrepreneur

The quintessential American hero is the self made millionaire—the entrepreneur. African-Americans even say the word with reverence—entrepreneur. These are the hardy souls who realized the American dream by overcoming odds that seemed insuperable.

Success as self-employed businessmen has been especially difficult for African-Americans because until recently they were unable to sell their products and services outside of the African-American community. Even when they were extremely profitable in this confined market, they offended European-Americans that found the competition unacceptable. Violence that was devastating to the African-Americans soon followed.

Between 1867 and 1917 the number of African-American businesses grew from 4,000 to 50,000. Affluent communities sprang up in several cities. Notable among these was Wilmington, North Carolina and Tulsa, Oklahoma. A riot in 1898 in Wilmington, directed at the business leaders, caused them to flee for their lives. Their businesses were quickly taken over by European-Americans.

In 1921 a similar assault wiped out the Greenwood section of Tulsa. This place was once called the black Wall Street. Greenwood had 30 restaurants, 15 doctors' offices, 5 hotels, 2 theaters, and 41 grocery stores and meat markets. The Tulsa riot burned to the ground 18,000 homes and businesses owned by African-Americans. More than 300 African-Americans were killed.

Wilmington and Tulsa had wide ranging riots. There are also many stories of businessmen who had to flee in the night for no reason other than that they were African-American and successful. It is no wonder, then, that with such a history, the African-American entrepreneur has attained a special status in the community.

Every year in its June issue *Black Enterprise* magazine reports on the largest African-American businesses. While the size of these businesses is small relative to companies listed in the Fortune magazine 500, it is still a great sign of hope to see the economic growth. According to *Black Enterprise*, the top 100 African-American businesses generated more than $20 Billion in sales in 2000.

It is little wonder that you might be motivated to join that illustrious group. But remember that no one writes great stories about those who failed. And their number is large. Even worse than the complete collapse of a business is one that limps along forever, adroitly avoiding death.

Before taking the plunge, be sure that you understand the pressures you will face. Do you have the energy to work 16 hour days, 7 days a week, while your business is getting started? Do you feel comfortable working without benefits, even a paycheck at times, without any perks that one expects in an established business? Is your family also willing to endure these hardships?

To be successful you will have to be an independent thinker with a great need to achieve. You will have to have the self confidence, the professional contacts and the business skills required in the industry you have chosen.

Even if you do everything right, an unexpected downturn in the economy could frustrate your timetable for profitability. But if you have the courage to endure through all this adversity, establishing a highly successful business is the best way to get rich if you don't sing, dance or slam-dunk.

-10-
The Hidden Enemy

There is a hidden enemy that works incessantly against you becoming rich. That enemy is called "inflation." You probably thought that was a problem only for the big-money people, but inflation is something that you have to keep in mind as you develop your plan to get rich.

When the price of gasoline or heating fuel takes a sudden jump, that is something with an immediate impact on your household budget. But you tend to treat that as an unfortunate but unusual event. You do not notice that most consumer prices have been creeping up over time. If you have been fortunate enough to be promoted or to earn salary raises you have more income so you are less likely to notice the price increases.

Over a period of time the change is extraordinary. When I graduated from college in 1956, the minimum wage was

$1.00 per hour. A person earning the minimum wage would get $40 a week, $2,080 a year. Today the minimum wage is $5.15 per hour. That comes to $206 a week and $10,712 a year.

Your first reaction was probably shock that the minimum wage could have been only $1.00 an hour in 1956. In today's economy a dollar does not go very far. But back in 1956 a dollar was worth much more. Every year the Employment Standards Administration of the U.S. Department of Labor prepares a Consumer Price Index (CPI). This enables a comparison of the cost of living from one year to another.

When one compares the $1.00 an hour in 1956 with the CPI in 1996, that $1.00 has the same buying power as $5.77 in 1996. In terms of buying power, the minimum wage in 1956 was actually worth more than the current $5.15. That is worth only $4.72 in buying power at the 1996 standard.

Always remember that the objective in getting rich is to acquire substantial future buying power.

Inflation is the national tendency for consumer prices to increase. Since 1925 the rate of increase in the United States has averaged 3% per year. Sometimes it is more, sometimes it is less. But what that rate tells you is that if your investments do not earn at least 3% net on average, then you are losing buying power.

Unless you read the business pages of the newspaper you might not even be aware of inflation. While some prices are rising, others are going down. For example, the price of computers and other technologically based products tend to fall as innovation goes forward. Nonetheless, the CPI never falls, but sometimes the increase is minimal.

Some prices rise much faster than the CPI and can create quite a problem. In some sections of the country the jump in real estate values has caused senior citizens considerable difficulty. In their youth, a husband and wife may have bought a nice house in a stable neighborhood for $20,000. They expected to pay off the mortgage and live out their lives in the homestead.

Over the years their stable neighborhood became fashionable and real estate values soared. Now the house they bought for $20,000 is worth $450,000. The mortgage is paid off but the real estate taxes at the appreciated value cost more than the mortgage. They did not plan to be hit with an expense like that after their retirement.

People tend to become emotionally attached to their home-stead. There are always so many family memories. But the financially wiser course of action would be to sell the house. With the family grown the parents probably need less space. Buy another house or condo with the proceeds from the sale and use the balance to add to your investment account.

Another soaring expense that hits families even earlier is the cost of private education. When I was at Harvard $5,000 a year would be more than enough for tuition, room and board and sundry expenses at any Ivy League school. Now it costs four times that for a quality private elementary day school. For private, high end colleges, $30,000 a year is needed now for expenses. And who knows what the tariff will be when your child is ready for college.

While the general rate of inflation has been 3%, the cost of college education has been rising at a 5% annual rate. It will take a well considered strategy to develop a plan for the education of your children.

You can cope with inflation while you are working. The level of salaries will usually be adjusted to the increased cost of living. But what will you do once you retire and are living on a fixed income. Social Security makes cost of living adjustments, but as you well know there are problems with the social security program. Who knows what will be available when you reach 65.

At an annual rate of inflation of 3% it will take about 24 years for the cost of living to double. You must assume, when developing your plan, that you will live long enough for inflation to be a factor even in retirement.

One lesson you should learn from inflation is that you should not save cash in a box under the bed. Every year savings in that box will lose 3% of its buying power. Your objective must be to invest in something that will appreciate in value at a rate greater than the rate of inflation.

The classic way to beat inflation is to have a portion of your funds invested in stocks. As inflation grows the cost of doing business will increase. Companies will be forced to raise their prices. As a result the dollar amount of their profits will grow and this will tend to increase the value of the companies' stock prices.

As you develop your get rich plan, always keep in mind that inflation is constantly working to reduce the buying power of your growing nest egg.

"When we were young we sacrificed to invest, but look at us now."

–11–
Asset Management

Back in the old days when you were a spend thrift the idea of money management had little significance. It meant only managing your paycheck to the bank to cover the checks you had already written to pay your bills. But now it means something else. Every week your nest egg has grown fatter. After a while you begin to understand that you have to make some serious decisions about how to handle these resources.

You know that you do not want to keep all of your funds in a checking account where it draws little interest. So the first thing you want to do is decide how much cash you want to keep readily accessible in a checking account. As you adjust the size of your checking account deposit, make sure that your balance will remain large enough to assure you cost-free checking.

Place the balance of the cash you want to be quickly available in a money market account where it draws more interest. Usually both types of account are available at the same bank. If not there are money market mutual funds.

If after making this adjustment you still have considerable savings it is time to consider investment. For most people the biggest asset they own is their residence. If you have been renting, it might be time to consider buying a place. Many people think of this as consumption because it is personal; but it is really an investment. A piece of real estate is relatively permanent while whatever is classified as a consumer item has a short useful life.

It is part of the American dream to own your home. Many emotions are involved in making the decision where to buy, when to buy, and how much to spend. People often get carried away. Fortunately, their bank will not grant a mortgage with payments that exceed your capacity to pay.

In the middle-income range you will spend about one-third of your gross income on housing. For example, if your household income were $55,000 you would spend about $18,150 a year on shelter. That is a large number. Just think of how quickly your savings/investment funds would grow if you could save on this item. However, you might not want to change your life style to save on your housing expense.

Americans are accustomed to the luxury of having relatively large residences. This was not always the case. Decades ago large families lived in small apartments. Bedrooms were lined with bunkbeds, and there was little open space. Even now I notice that several immigrant families will share an apartment to save on the rent.

It is unlikely that you would be willing to accept such spartan accommodations when you have the financial resources to afford greater comfort. Nonetheless, it is important to have a clear perspective on your housing needs. As a graduate of Harvard College and Columbia Law School I found it necessary to give up my comfortable apartment and become a roomer when starting a business. With housing costs rising, it is important for you to consider what sacrifices your household is willing to make to hold costs in check.

As a renter you simply pay the funds to the landlord as rent. The landlord will have the responsibility for maintaining the property. Or you can buy your own home and pay the money to the bank, which holds the mortgage. So where is the savings you ask?

It happens because of the tax law. If you had a mortgage of $200,000 at 7.5% interest for 30 years your monthly payment would be $1398. That comes to $16,781 for the year. However, $14,937 of this in the first year is for interest. When paying your income taxes you can deduct the interest payment and local real estate taxes from your income. You would save whatever the taxes would have been on the funds you used to pay those bills. That would probably amount to about $5,000. That would be a significant addition to your savings/investment account.

The strategy can work well as long as you remember the three most important factors in real estate. They are location, location, location. You want to be careful to buy in an area where the real estate values are likely to be at least stable over the years. Inflation will tend to push up real estate values as long as the neighborhood remains sound.

One of the greatest advantages of owning rather than renting is that you will be building an asset as you pay down your mortgage. When you rent it's the landlord who gets the asset. Many families plan to buy a house and pay off the mortgage by the time of retirement so that housing costs will be substantially reduced. They also will have the value of the house as an asset for extreme emergencies and as part of their estate to bequeath to their children.

It is not necessary for the objective of every investment to maximize profits. Personal satisfaction is certainly an important consideration. The purchase of a home is one such investment. But never forget it is indeed an investment. If the neighborhood is questionable, be certain that you are paying a discounted price for the quality of the house you are buying. You must be satisfied that your house will at least sustain its value for the years that you intend to own it.

Some find the business strategy of owning real estate so attractive that they decide to buy a multi-family building. The economics of such a concept are a little different. The idea is to live in one apartment and rent the others. Ideally, the rent from the other units will be sufficient to cover the mortgage and the operating costs for the whole building. The owner will then be able to live there free. Of course he must have the temperament to cope with sometimes irate tenants and be responsible for the upkeep of the premises.

The sales price of a multi-unit building will ordinarily be greater than the price for a single family. Banks will issue a mortgage based, in part, upon the expected rental income from the building. Nonetheless, the buyer will have to make a much larger down payment. When evaluating the business advantage of such a project it is well to consider what other investments for the additional down payment are available.

The single family house I used as example earlier had a mortgage of $200,000. Assume also that the multi-family building has a mortgage of $400,000 with a down payment of $40,000. The question, then, is what is the best investment of the extra $20,000. If the investment period is 30 years, the same term as a mortgage, the return from a growth stock mutual fund could be much greater than the appreciated value of the real estate.

In the world of stock investments 30 years is a very long time. An investment 0f $20,000 with an average quarterly compound interest rate of 15% would be worth $1,658,069 in 30 years. In order to equal that return from the original investment, the value of the real estate would have to increase by 380% in 30 years.

It is certainly possible for the real estate to increase in value in the same way. Those skilled in predicting population shifts have made fortunes in real estate. The downside is that the area could deteriorate and the building is worth less or little more than you paid for it. After 30 years of your hard work in maintaining the property that would be a very disappointing result.

With the investment of the $20,000 in a mutual fund there would be no additional effort required of you. One of the advantages of stock investment, your money does the work.

The Stock Market

The classic concept of a rich individual is one who has fat dividend checks mailed to his or her mansion every quarter. The only effort required of them is to go to the bank to deposit the checks. The stock market is the place where fortunes are made. In order to get rich you will have to invest some of your assets there.

The stock market remains an unfathomable mystery to most people. There is no way that I will be able to unravel the mystery satisfactorily in this brief guide. The most that I can hope for is to raise some of the important issues for you to consider.

The two primary investment instruments are stocks and bonds. Stocks give you a share of ownership in a business while bonds are a certificate of indebtedness. If there are 1,000,000 shares of common stock in a business and you own 100,000, then you own 10% of the business. However, if you own a $100,000 bond which pays 8% interest, then the company must pay you $8,000 every year until they repay you the $100,000 on the stipulated date.

The value of stocks will fluctuate up and down with changes in the company's profitability, and the value of bonds will fluctuate in accordance with the level of interest rates in the economy. But none of these factors should concern you because you will undoubtedly be investing in mutual funds or with the advice of a financial advisor. They are the ones to be concerned about the economic conditions in the market.

Your concern should be on your investment objectives. You have already decided how much to keep in your checking account and how much to keep in a money market account. Other goals might be the education of children, retirement, or simply the building of assets. Tax considerations will play an important role in maximizing the results of your various objectives.

The factors that will influence your investment strategy will be how much time you have before you have to meet certain financial obligations, and how much money you have available for investment. The longer the period of time the better. In the long run an aggressive growth stock fund will provide the greatest return. However, the short term value of such investments is unpredictable.

One of the most promising retirement investments is the 401 (k) plan. This permits you to deduct up to 15% of your gross pay up to a maximum of $10,500. So your taxable income is reduced by the amount of your investment. Usually the employer matches all or a portion of what you invest. This is equivalent to getting a tax free pay increase. You will usually have a choice from a number of investment plans which are managed by professional money managers.

Assume that your annual salary is $40,000 and you have $200 per month deducted for your 401(k) Plan. That is $2,400 per year, 6% of your salary. If you have a generous employer who matches your contribution up to 6% of your salary, then another $2,400 per year would be invested in your account. After 15 years at a 12% average annual rate of return, you would have $201,830 and you would have invested only $36,000.

It is important to understand the magic of compounding. That happens when the money your investment earns makes money. The longer your money is at work its growth becomes exponential. If the same plan described above was implemented for 30 years and earned the same rate of return, the size of the pot would be huge. Instead of $201,830 after 15 years it would be $1,411,966 at the end of 30.

The longer period of time would permit even more aggressive investments so it is not unreasonable to assert that the average rate of compound interest would be 15%. In that case the value of the investment would be $2,803,928. It is reasonable to assert that anyone holding almost $3 million in assets is rich.

At retirement time you would convert your holdings into a more conservative portfolio. Withdrawing income at the rate of 5% a year would provide a retirement income of more than $140,196. That would easily place you at a comfortable level of income.

One of the advantages of the 401(k) Plan is that you can invest up to 15% of your earnings, and that amount will be deducted from your W-2 for tax purposes. In addition, your employer can contribute up to 6% of your annual income. Furthermore, the value of your investment account can increase without tax consequences.

When you reach retirement age and deduct money from your account for living expenses, you will then pay taxes at the income tax rate prevailing at the time. If you change jobs prior to retirement you can rollover your 401(k) Plan into another plan with your new employer or into an IRA.

There are other employer retirement plans which operate very much like the 401(k). Prominent among these are the SEP IRA and the Simple IRA. I will not discuss their details here. Just remember that the significant features are that your contribution is tax deductible, that your interests vest within a short time, and that the policy of the company is to contribute to your plan.

When looking for a new job, if there are several opportunities which appear to be equally promising, you should make a careful study of the different employee benefit plans. Look beyond health and hospitalization to evaluate the companies' retirement plans. Always keep in mind that when the company matches your retirement savings, it's like a raise that never appears on your W-2 tax form.

You are never too young to start your plan to get rich. The more time your investments have to grow the better. If your company does not offer a retirement plan, then start your own. A ROTH IRA or a regular IRA provides certain tax benefits. But remember that once you put money away for retirement in a plan with tax benefits, you will be penalized if you cash it in before age 59 ½. You can borrow from a 401 (k).

It would be wonderful to get rich when you are young. You could buy flashy cars—more than one at that. You could party with the rich and prominent. You might even become famous. All that is very nice. Who would begrudge you those luxuries if they were acquired with surplus funds. But the real point of getting rich is to be able to enjoy a comfortable life style when you get old.

Four in 10 Americans over age 60 will experience poverty at some time in their later years. Have you noticed some very old people bagging groceries or working as waitstaff or security guards. Some work to keep busy but others work for survival. A sound plan for retirement begun in your youth will enable you to get rich and have a comfortable old age. It is not too late to start at age 50. But the investment will have to be substantial to enable you to build the required resources.

One expense that sidetracks young families is the cost of educating their children. An education ERA or a 529 Plan offer tax benefits for a fund which can be used only for the education of children. If you put away $100 a month when a child was born, and continued this for 18 years, at 12% compound interest the fund would be worth $76,544 when the child is ready for college.

It is a personal decision as to how much to invest for education. From a cold blooded perspective, such diversion of funds will reduce the amount of your wealth in your old age. But loving parents are willing to make a sacrifice. It would be unwise, however, to postpone entirely your get rich plan.

"We'll watch the game in a minute. I just have to see how my stocks are doing."

-12-

The Next Generation

You are aware of how important your education and skills have been for your success. It is only natural, then, that you would want to provide even greater educational opportunities for your children. Some people mistakenly look at the cost of higher education and throw their hands up in despair. Since the cost seems out of reach, they fail to motivate their children to achieve academically and develop their talents.

A better strategy is to begin the process of education from the birth of your child. Not only will it be an expression of your love for your child, but it will also pay off in the long run as your child becomes academically proficient at a young age. Who knows, when you look at your baby, what talents there are that will earn your child a scholarships to college?

There are many theories about techniques for early child rearing, and I will not presume to propose one system over another. I am certainly not qualified to do so. But I do claim that a solid foundation in the english language is a gift that your child will always treasure. It is never too early to start reading to your child every day. As he or she gets older you simply read age-appropriate books that get more complicated with the age of the child. Once you establish a love of learning and language, academic competency for your child is assured provided there are adequate schools.

A reading habit can be very expensive if you buy all the books you read. If you live in a place with a good public library you will be able to find all of the books you will need. And it's free.

Since this is a book on how to get rich what does all of this information about child rearing have to do with acquiring wealth? Everything. One of the biggest expenses of your middle-age years will be the education of your children. You must begin planning for this at the earliest opportunity. If effective child rearing practices could save you thousands of dollars later, that is certainly an appropriate consideration for your get rich plan.

Some believe it is enough to focus on providing funds for college. That is certainly necessary, but it would be a mistake to have a casual attitude about primary and secondary school. I read recently about a family in Chicago that sent all of their children to a local parochial school that maintained high academic standards. It was financially challenging for the parents to afford the tuition for their many children, but they believed the soundness of the early education was most important. The children were then expected to provide for their own higher education.

Many African-American families face this dilemma. Urban public education in America is notoriously deficient. The question you must answer is whether you should send your child to public school, or like the Chicago family, pay for private or parochial school. Tuition at private day schools has soared around the country so that private secondary school is more expensive than tuition at some state colleges.

Another strategy might be to move to a community that has good public schools. The additional cost for housing might be less than the tuition for your children in private school. The advantage of this solution is that the money is being spent to build value in an asset—your home.

A move to a more affluent suburb with good schools is not an option for many because of cost. The recent census showed that most major cities are becoming even more racially segregated for children. Topping the list are: Detroit, MI; Milwaukee, WI; New York, NY; Newark, NJ; Chicago, IL; Cleveland, OH; Miami, Cincinnati, OH; Birmingham, AL; and St. Louis, MO. Strangely enough, some of the least segregated cities for children are now in the south, and include: Norfolk, VA; Charleston, SC; Augusta, GA; Greenville, SC; Raleigh-Durham, NC; Jacksonville, FL; and Columbia, SC. There is some evidence that the more segregated the student body the fewer the resources committed to education.

Wherever your children go to school, it will be important for you to be actively involved in their education if primarily as a cheerleader. It is natural to want to see your children succeed, but it is also money in the bank when scholarships are awarded.

You cannot plan on your children earning athletic or academic scholarships to cover the cost of college education. Your success in implementing your get rich plan might also push you into an income and asset category that diminishes the possibility of getting scholarships available for students from economically deprived families. The best strategy is to develop a college education plan.

Investment in the college education of your children is a great financial sacrifice for parents. That money invested in a good growth fund could provide a great nest egg for retirement. But that is a sacrifice most parents are willing to make to ease the way for the next generation.

Nonetheless, it is appropriate to be realistic about what you can afford. If there are several children, it might not be possible for you to finance room, board and tuition at a major private university. That costs about $30,000 a year now. Heaven knows what the tariff will be when your children are ready for college. You must develop a plan and determine what you can invest on a regular basis to finance that plan.

The average annual cost for a four-year private U.S. college is $22,533 and $10,458 for a public college. This includes tuition, room, board, fees and books. At those rates it would cost $90,132 for four years at a private college and $41,832 at a public school. Those are big numbers but they will get even bigger if college costs continue to grow at an average of 5% per year as they have recently. In 15 years, four years at a private college would cost $187,378 and four years at a public school would be $86,966.

The good news is that the quality of public colleges has greatly improved. The University of North Carolina at Chapel Hill, the University of Michigan, the University of Massachusetts at Amherst, the University of California at Berkeley, and Cal Tech are all academically superior to most private colleges. You could plan to send two children to public colleges for the same cost as sending one to a private school.

The various states have established tax-deferred investment plans, permitted under section 529 of the Internal Revenue Code, to enable you to save for college expenses. These investment plans are administered by professional investment managers, and the money is invested in mutual funds. You can invest in such a plan for as little as $50 per month.

There are two significant tax advantages of such plans. The first is that there are no taxes on dividends or profits from the sale of stocks which the investment manager might realize. So the fund grows tax free. The second is that distributions from the fund are now not taxed so long as they are used to pay legitimate education expenses such as tuition, room and board, books and fees.

You will be able to select from a number of investment funds which will be riskier or more conservative, depending upon the length of time you have before your child goes to college. For example, if you invest $200 a month in a fund that earns an annual rate of 8%, you will have invested $12,000 in five years and it would be worth $14,588. But if you had started the plan early enough and could invest $200 a month for 15 years, you would have invested $36,000 and it would be worth $67,521. The longer the time the more the magic of compounding has effect.

There is a limit on how much an individual can give in one year. Federal gift taxes will be incurred for investments of more than $50,000. There is also a limit on the total amount that can be contributed to each plan. That is determined by the cost of education in that state. In Massachusetts, for example, the maximum is $171,125. This number will be adjusted as the cost of education increases.

The fund will remain under your control, and you have the right to designate another beneficiary. However, you cannot switch the fund to another investment program once you have selected a plan. And you can not withdraw funds from the plan except for a qualified use without incurring a tax penalty.

Of course there are expenses for administering the plan. These would vary from state to state. In Massachusetts there is a $30 annual account fee. In addition there is an annual fee of 0.7% of the asset value of each portfolio and a 0.3% administration fee. So the expenses amount to $30 plus 1.0% of the asset value of the fund each year.

You need not be a resident of a state to enroll in the 529 plan of that state. All U.S. residents may participate. A 529 plan is an excellent way for grand parents to contribute to the education of their grandchildren without incurring any gift taxes.

There is also an Education IRA under Section 530 of the Internal Revenue Code which was not used very much. There was an investment limit of $500 and it was not available to more affluent families. The recent tax cut law has amended the Education IRA to make it more attractive. Most of the investment went to the 529 accounts. It remains to be seen how effective the changes in the Education IRA will be.

For information on every 529 Plan in the country, look up the College Savings Plan network on their website, www.collegesavings.org. Some states even allow a tax deduction on the funds contributed.

"It's amazing how interested you get in Wall Street when your own money is in play."

–13–
Strategy For Success

For many people the stock market is a scary place. The prospect of making a lot of money is enticing. But then there are terrible crashes which wipe out billions in value in one day. In order to feel comfortable about your investment plan, it is important to understand how the investment strategy works to enable your plan to succeed.

The first factor is time. Research shows that almost any 30 year period of the market has been marked by positive growth. That is why it is so important to start your plan as early as possible to maximize the time you are invested.

Secondly, by investing in a mutual fund or a professionally managed pool, you will immediately achieve portfolio diversity. The fund will be invested in a substantial number of stocks and they will not have all their eggs in one basket. One or several poorly performing stocks will not seriously damage the fund's results.

Thirdly, by investing periodically you will be "dollar cost averaging." The goal in stock investment is to buy low and sell high. But no one knows for certain precisely what those values are. By investing in the fund systematically you will sometimes buy low and other times buy high, but the average will tend to be a reasonable price.

There are many different kinds of funds. For investors who can wait a long time for a good return there are aggressive growth funds. These will provide the best rate of return over many years but their values are unpredictable in the short run.

Then there are more balanced funds which contain bonds and more conservative stocks. Their short term values are more predictable but they will not usually give you the net worth appreciation possible with growth funds.

Of course there are too many other types of investment funds to discuss in this guide. The point is that there are carefully thought out investment strategies to guard against catastrophic loss in value. As your circumstances change it may be appropriate to shift from a dynamic growth fund to one that is more conservative. As you approach retirement you will want to secure the appreciation in value you have gained over the years.

For someone who has had little experience with the stock market it is advisable to have a certified financial advisor. If your retirement plan is through your place of employment, the company will have undoubtedly engaged the services of an advisor for the company plan. You will have to obtain an advisor for the other aspects of your plan.

Those who have some money left after establishing the mutual funds for their plan, and have some interest in learning more about investments, I suggest they join the American Association of Individual Investors. The AAII is located at 625 N. Michigan Avenue, Chicago, IL 60611. The telephone number is (312) 280-0170.

–14–
The Mutual Fund

As an inexperienced stock market investor you will undoubtedly make your initial investments in mutual funds. It makes sense, therefore, to have a clear understanding of what a mutual fund is and how it works.

Before mutual funds were established, extremely wealthy industrialists would hire private investment managers to invest their profits in other promising companies. Private banks also offered the service of managing investment portfolios for their wealthy clients. A substantial investment was necessary to avail oneself of these services.

Then one imaginative fellow realized that if the goal was to accumulate assets, it made no difference whether one person invested one million dollars or one hundred people invested

$10,000 each. The only difference was the clerical complexity of managing so many different accounts.

Thus the mutual fund was born. Investors place their funds with professional investment managers who acquire stocks, bonds or other securities which are mutually owned by the investors. It is quite simple to determine how many shares of the fund any subsequent investor can own. The managers determine the market value of all the securities the fund owns and divide that sum by the number of shares owned by the investors. That figure is called the net asset value or NAV.

If the market value of all the securities was $100,000,000 and there were 10,000,000 shares outstanding, then the NAV would be $10. So if you wanted to invest $1,000 into that fund you would get 100 shares. But that is only if that was what is called a no-load fund, one that has no sales charge. If it is a load fund with a sales charge, the price of each share would be quoted as the maximum offering price or the MOP. That would be the NAV plus the sales charge.

The type of mutual funds discussed so far are called open-end funds. That is they remain open to new investors. There are also closed-end funds which are priced on the stock exchange just like any other listed company. Their prices will fluctuate at the whim of the market. These are not the mutual funds in which you will be investing, but it is good to know about them.

The reason that professional investment advisor services were available only to the very wealthy in the past is that fees are usually a small percentage of the assets in the fund. In a billion dollar fund, an annual fee of 0.5% is $5,000,000. But if the size of the fund is only ten million dollars, the fee would be only $50,000, hardly enough to pay management expenses.

Before investing in a fund you should get the prospectus and review it although the task might seem imposing. The prospectus will tell you what the management fee is, whether there are distribution fees, or 12b-1 fees for marketing and advertising expenses, and what the sales charges are when you buy or sell.

There are now thousands of mutual funds from which to choose. Investment companies will have a large number of mutual funds, all with different investment strategies. One advantage of choosing a family of funds is that as your investment needs change you can often transfer from one fund to another without paying an additional sales fee. The prospectus will indicate what the terms are. Appendix H lists a number of fund families and their telephone numbers.

With so many funds to choose from it might be difficult for you to decide without sound advice. That is why some funds have sales fees. These fees compensate the financial advisor for his services in helping you to get into the right fund for you. Even so, it is important to review the prospectus and the past performance of a fund before you invest.

There are a number of factors which will determine what funds are suitable for you. How long can you stay invested before you will need cash? Do you need some income now? How much risk can you tolerate? Will the swings of the market and the drop in the value of your investment disturb you?

The longer you can stay invested the riskier your portfolio can be, provided you feel comfortable with the occasional drops in value. If you will need income soon, then a portfolio with stocks and bonds might be more desirable. The bonds will tend to mute the swings in value of the stocks and will provide income.

You can arrange with the fund to send you dividend and interest checks or you can have the funds reinvest the money. Whether you get a check in the mail or reinvest the money your tax liability will be the same. If you transfer from one fund in a family to another you may incur tax liability in the process. There may be some stocks in the portfolio that have grown in value. When you transfer funds, the IRS will consider that to be the same as a sale, so you will incur capital gains liability.

The major advantage of a mutual fund is that for a small investment you will acquire an interest in a diversified portfolio. You avoid the risk of putting all your eggs in one basket. In a well managed stock fund a few stocks will be big winners, most will perform adequately, and there will be a few dogs. A competent manager should be quick to eliminate the dogs and should be astute enough to pick some big winners.

If you are on a regular investment plan you will have resolved the most trying dilemma faced by an investor, when is the best time to buy. The ideal is to buy low and sell high, but no one knows precisely when those points are reached. Dollar cost averaging gives you a good average price. When you invest the same amount every month you will buy more shares when the price is low and fewer when it is high, but you will end up with a good average price for your shares.

Mutual funds provide you with the same services of professional investment advisors that were once available only to the very wealthy. The choices are vast as you can see from the list of fund families in Appendix H.

–15–
Insurance

I must say a few words about another important financial concern—life insurance. When most African-Americans think about life insurance they are primarily concerned with having enough funds to provide a proper burial. When you set foot on the road to becoming rich you are beyond that. You have to think of insurance as another element of your investment strategy.

If you are the breadwinner of your family your primary insurance concern will be to provide financial support for the family in the event of your untimely death. You would want to provide funds to pay off the mortgage, educate the children, and pay daily living expenses. Of course there should also be enough to pay for the funeral.

Financial advisors would suggest a policy large enough to cover 7 or 10 times your annual income. Of course the necessary amount will vary from person to person. Someone without dependents might want only enough insurance to pay his or her estate taxes.

One of the advantages of insurance is that the proceeds are not included in the estate of the deceased. When you consider that the estate tax takes half of the assets above the exemption amount, an investment in insurance is a practical way to circumvent that problem.

There are many different types of life insurance plans. I do not intend to discuss them here. I will point out only that the basic type of insurance is called term life. For a fixed premium the insurer will pay the policy benefit to the beneficiary if the insured dies during the term of the policy.

More complex are the whole life policies and their derivatives. The premium for this kind of policy is higher, but there is an investment aspect to the policy. After a while the insured will accrue cash surrender values in this type of policy. Sometime the earnings from the policy will pay future premiums.

You will have to decide what insurance, if any, is appropriate for you. An easy way to learn what the rates are at your age from competing companies look up www.quotesmith.com on the internet.

–16–
Your Financial Advisor

Now that you have developed your plan and have accumulated some savings, it is time to make a most critical decision that will profoundly affect your future financial success. It is time to select a financial planner.

Unless you have taken investment courses and studied the market assiduously you will not be qualified to make the best decisions about investments. Because of the broad based success in the long running bull market, some people have concluded that it is easy to be an effective investor. It is not. Select a financial planner.

There is no doubt that you will be investing in mutual funds, but which ones. Appendix H lists the names of some of the major fund families. There are many families and each can have as many as 80 different mutual funds. You can call the toll free number and order information on those funds which interest you. It will require some expertise to select the best fund for you and your family.

Now that you have read most of this book, you should have a working knowledge of the issues involved in making financial planning decisions. You are by no means an expert but you certainly know enough to help you evaluate a professional. There is no single accrediting institution as there is for doctors and lawyers to give you confidence in your selection. As a result it is difficult to say with certainty who or what is a bona fide financial planner.

There are several organizations that have certifying programs. They are the Certified Financial Planner Board of Standards (CFP) located in Denver. A telephone call to them at 888-237-6275 will get you a list of professionals in your area. There is also the National Association of Personal Financial Advisors (NAPFA) at 847-537-7722 and the International Association for Financial Planning (IAFP) at 800-945-4237.

In addition to these organizations major financial institutions may have their own internal training programs that will prepare their employees for the different qualifying examinations of the National Association of Security Dealers (NASD). A financial specialist will have to be certified by the NASD as a broker-dealer in order to transact business on his own.

The most common way people find a financial planner is by a referral from a friend. Or sometimes you might meet someone at a social event who it turns out is a financial advisor. While such contacts will let you know whether you enjoy this person's company, it will require more for you to trust him or her with your wealth.

The first test for me would be whether the financial planner is part of a financially strong organization such as John Hancock, Fidelity, The Advest Group, Merrill Lynch or some other similar company. There are two reasons for this. The first is that as part of a major financial institution your advisor would have access to the best research available.

The second reason concerns financial responsibility. If your advisor should negligently or fraudulently suggest investments that have disastrous results, a financially strong company will make good. It is unlikely that an independent financial planner would have the resources or the willingness to cover his negligent decisions.

Of course there are many independent financial planners who are very competent. Nonetheless, planners with a major financial institution are just as good and they have substantial research and economic back up. But regardless of who they are, I would first check to determine whether any complaints have been filed against them. Check with the Securities and Exchange Commission in Washington, DC at 202-942-4320. Or you can call your regional office of the SEC listed in Appendix I. Also check with the NASD at 800-289-999 if your advisor is a broker-dealer.

If you have not met a financial advisor and are ready for the service, you should call one of the associations listed above for names of advisors in your area. Tell them that you are interested only in those associated with large financial institutions.

Talk with several until you find one who meets your requirements.

You have your plan. You know what you want to accomplish. Have each candidate hoping to become your financial planner spell out in detail what he or she would propose. Learn what the relationship would be after the initial investments have been made. Determine whether there is good chemistry between you and the person who might become your financial planner.

A most important aspect of your search is to learn what prospective financial planners charge for their services. For those who can afford to entrust substantial sums to the advisors, the answer is relatively simple. The advisor will charge an annual fee usually paid quarterly. But for those with more modest resources the method of payment is considerably more complex. The financial advisor will have to generate his or her revenue from commissions he earns from the investments or insurance bought for your account. There is some inducement, therefore, for an unscrupulous advisor to put you into investments which are not the best for you but pay the most to the advisor.

Knowledge is the best defense you have against being misled. The law requires financial advisors to file form ADV either with the state or with federal authorities. There are two parts to the form and you should ask to see them both. Part I lists the investment instruments the advisor sells. Part II lists the advisor's qualifications and the fees that are charged.

Another source for information about selecting an advisor is free from TIAA-CREF. Its title is "Choosing A Financial

Planner." Call 800-842-2733 and ask for the publication department.

Remember you are the client, the customer. Use your common-sense and be tough.

Postscript

We as African-Americans have come a long way. The road has been full of ruts and sharp turns. There have been many obstacles along the way, but we have persevered. After decades of struggle from the end of slavery in 1865, the legal framework for racial equality was established with the passage of the Civil Rights Act of 1964 and the Voting Rights Act of 1965.

It did not take a rocket scientist to understand that it was discriminatory to require African-Americans to ride in the back of the bus. It was clearly racially abusive to force African-American children to attend inferior segregated schools. It was an obvious violation of the 14th Amendment of the U.S. Constitution to use force to prevent African-Americans from voting.

The focus of the Civil Rights Movement was always on the social injustice of racial discrimination. Little was said of the economic injustice. African-Americans who rode on the back of the bus and had to give up their seats as European-American passengers filed from the front paid the same fare as European-Americans. African-American children who were forced to attend inferior schools were educationally impaired and less qualified than European-Americans for better paying jobs. African-Americans denied the vote were unable to elect public officials who would assure that they received the many benefits provided by government.

The economic injustice of American apartheid was rarely discussed, except to point out that a disproportionate number of African-American families had incomes below the poverty level. Even then it was subtly suggested that African-American poverty was self inflicted. European-American society took no responsibility for African-American conduct which developed as a desperate refuge from the pain and anguish of racial discrimination.

In this new millennium it is time for African-Americans to direct their attention to the real challenges which lie ahead. We must understand that we have won the battle for Civil Rights. Of course, there will always be some recalcitrant European-Americans who want to turn back the clock. Our lawyers will see them in court. We must not be distracted from the job ahead.

African-Americans will never attain real freedom, justice and equality until we develop economic and political power. The issue is not to worry only about eliminating poverty. As is stated in the Book of Matthew (26:11) the poor will always be with us. The issue is to build African-American wealth. Hand in hand with that goal is the development of political power as a means to secure our prosperity.

The poverty mindset that has been so carefully cultivated among us is a great impediment to our economic progress. Too many of us mistakenly believe that they are poor and must remain so. "How to Get Rich When You Ain't Got Nothing'" sets forth how every individual must start the process for acquiring wealth. It is a process available to everyone. You don't need a leader, an economic Martin Luther King, to lead you toward wealth.

There is some social action you would be wise to include in your plan. Think of yourself as empowered. Become knowledgeable on political issues and become politically active. I don't mean just to vote. My father used to say, "Any fool can vote. You have to become involved even earlier in the process." Remember that government policy has a great impact on the development of wealth.

Whenever possible support African-American businesses and professionals. One important business institution that deserves your support is the Boston Bank of Commerce, and their affiliates. They have a strategy of uniting African-American banks across the country to create a financial institution of significant size. They are already in Boston, Miami and Los Angeles. Such a bank will be able to assist African-American entrepreneurs when other institutions turn their back.

Be prepared to participate in boycotts of European-American businesses and institutions that fail to serve African-Americans properly. Boycotts were used effectively in the civil rights movement and may be resorted to again.

Most of all, understand that you are a great being who deserves the best. I hope that this book changes the way you think about yourself and your opportunities. With the right attitude and determination you can attain what you will.

Appendixes

Appendix A

State Directors of Adult Education

If you have difficulty at your state office then contact the Federal headquarters at Clearinghouse on Adult Education and Literacy, Division of Adult Education and Literacy, U.S. Department of Education, 400 Maryland Ave., SW, Washington, DC 20202; 202-205-9996.

Alabama
State Administrator
GED Testing Program
Adult Basic Education Section
Division of Federal Administrative Services
Department of Education
Gordon Parsons Building, Rm. 5343
50 North Ripley Street
Montgomery, AL 36130
334-242-8181
Fax: 334-242-2236

Alaska
State Supervisor, Adult Basic Education
Department of Education
801 West 10th, Box F
Funeau, AK 99801
907-465-3396

Arizona
State Administrator
Adult Education Services
Department of Education
1535 West Jefferson
Phoenix, AR 85007
602-542-1849

Arkansas
Deputy Director
Adult Education Section
Department of Education
Luther S. Hardin Building, #506
Third Capitol Mall
Little Rock, AR 72201-1083
501-682-1970/1978
Fax: 501-682-1982

California
State Director
Adult Education
Department of Education
P.O. Box 944272
Sacramento, CA 942244-2720
916-322-6535
Fax: 916-327-4239

Colorado
State Director, ABE
Division of Adult Education
201 E. Colfax Avenue
Denver, CO 80203
303-866-6611
Fax: 303-830-0793

Connecticut
Director, Division of Vocational
   Technical and Adult Education
Department of Education
25 Industrial Park Rd.
Middletown, CT 06457
203-638-4035
Fax: 203-638-4156/4062

Delaware
State Supervisor
Adult and Community Education
Department of Public Instruction
P.O. Box 1402
J.G. Townsend Building
Dover, DE 19901
302-739-4681
Fax: 302-739-3744

District of Columbia
Assistant Superintendent
District of Columbia Public Schools
Browne Administrative Unit
26th and Benning Rd., NE
Washington, DC 20002
202-724-4178
Fax: 202-724-4750

Florida
Bureau of Adult and Community
   Education
FEC Building
Department of Education
325 W. Gains Street
Room 1244
Tallahassee, FL 32399-0400
904-487-4929
Fax: 904-487-6259

Georgia
Assistant Commissioner for Adult
   Literacy
Department of Technical and A.E.
1800 Centary Place
Atlanta, GA 30345-4304
404-679-1635
Fax: 404-679—1630

Hawaii
Administrator, Youth and Early
   Childhood Section
Department of Education
Hahaione Elementary School
595 Pepeekeo St., H-2
Honolulu, HI 96825
808-395-9451
Fax: 808-395-1826

Idaho
Director Adult Education
Department of Education
Len B. Jordon Office Building
650 W. State Street
Boise, ID 83720
208-334-2187
Fax: 208-334-2228

Illinois

Director of Adult Education
Adult, Vocational and Technical
    Education
State Board of Education
100 N. First St., E-439
Springfield, IL 62777
217-782-3370
Fax: 217-782-9224

Indiana

Director, Division of Adult
    Education
Department of Education
Room 229, State House
Indianapolis, IN 46204
317-232-0522
Fax: 317-232-9121

Iowa

Chief, Adult Education
Department of Education
Grimes State Office Building
Des Moines, IA 50319-0146
515-281-3671
Fax: 515-242-5988

Kansas

Director, Adult Education
Department of Education
120 East 10th Street
Topeka, KS 66612
913-296-3191
Fax: 913-296-7933

Kentucky

Office Head
Adult Education Services
Department of Adult and Technical
    Education
Capital Plaza Tower, 3rd Floor
500 Mero Street
Frankfort, KY 40601
502-564-5114
Fax: 502-564-5316

Louisiana

Director, Bureau of Adult and
    Community Education
Department of Education
P.O. Box 94064
Baton Rouge, LA 70804-9064
504-342-3510
Fax: 504-342-7316

Maine

Adult and Community Education
Department of Education
State House Station 23
Augusta, ME 04333
207-289-5854
Fax: 207-287-5894

Maryland

Adult Education and Literacy
    Services Branch
Division of Career Technology and
    Adult Learning, 3rd Floor
Maryland State Department of
    Education
200 West Baltimore Street
Baltimore, MD 21201
410-767-0162
Fax: 410-333-2379

Massachusetts

Adult and Community Service
Department of Education
350 Main Street, 4th Floor
Malden, MA 02148
617-388-3300 ext. 353
Fax: 617-388-3394

Michigan

Adult Extended Learning Services
Department of Education
P.O. Box 30008
Lansing, MI 48909
517-373-8425
Fax: 517-335-3630

Minnesota

Adult Basic Education
Department of Education
997 Capital Square Building
550 Cedar Street
St. Paul, MN 55101
612-296-8311
Fax: 612-297-5695

Mississippi

Director of Literacy
State Board for Community and
   Junior Colleges
Education and Research Center
3825 Ridgewood Road
Jackson, MS 39211
601-982-6344
Fax: 601-359-2326

Missouri

Director, Adult Education
Department of Elementary and
   Secondary Education
P.O. Box 480
Jefferson City, MO 65102
314-751-0887
Fax: 314-751-1179

Montana

Director, Adult Education
State of Public Instruction
Office of the State Superintendent
State Capitol Building
Helena, MT 59602
406-444-4443
Fax: 406-444-3924

Nebraska

Director, Adult and Community
   Education
Department of Education
301 Centennial Mall South
P.O. Box 94987
Lincoln, NE 68509
402-471-4807
Fax: 402-471-0117

Nevada

Adult Basic Education Consultant
State GED Administrator
Department of Education
Adult and Continuing Education
400 W. King Street
Capitol Complex
Carson City, NV 89710
702-687-3134
Fax: 702-687-5660

New Hampshire

Supervisor, ABE
Department of Education
101 Pleasant Street
Concord, NH 03301
603-271-6698
Fax: 603-271-1953

New Jersey

Director, A.E.
Department of Education
225 West State Street
Trenton, NJ 08625-0500
609-777-0577
Fax: 609-633-9825

New Mexico

State Director, ABE
Department of Education
Education Building
300 Don Gaspar
Santa Fe, NM 87501
505-827-6672
Fax: 505-827-6696

New York

Director, Division of Continuing
   Education
State Education Department
Washington Ave.
Albany, NY 12234
518-474-5808
Fax: 518-474-2801

North Carolina
Director, Continuing Education
Department of Community Colleges
200 West Jones
Raleigh, NC 27063-1337
919-733-4791
Fax: 919-733-0680

North Dakota
Director, Adult Education
Department of Public Instruction
600 Boulevard Avenue East
9th Floor, State Capitol Building
Bismarck, ND 58505-0440
701-224-2393/3600
Fax: 701-224-2461

Ohio
State Director, Adult Education
Department of Education
933 High Street, Suite 210
Worthington, OH 43085-4087
614-466-5015
Fax: 614-752-1640 z9466-2372)

Oklahoma
Director, Lifelong Learning
Department of Education
Oliver Hodge memorial Education
   Building
2500 N. Lincoln Blvd., Room 180
Oklahoma City, OK 73105-4599
405-521-3321
Fax: 405-521-6205

Oregon
Office of Assistant Commissioner
Community College Services
255 Capitol St., NE
Salem, OR 97310
503-378-8585
Fax: 503-378-8434

Pennsylvania
Director, Bureau of Adult, Basic and
   Literacy Education
Department of Education
333 Market Street, 6th Floor
Harrisburg, PA 17126-0333
717-787-5532
Fax: 717-783-5420

Puerto Rico
Asst. Secretary for Adult Education
Educational Extension
P.O. Box 759
Hato Rey, PR 00919
809-753-9211
Fax: 809-754-0843

Rhode Island
Adult Education Specialist
Department of Education
22 Hayes St., Room 222
Roger Williams Building
Providence, RI 02908
401-277-2705
Fax: 401-277-6033

South Carolina
State Director
Office of Community Education
South Carolina Department of
   Education
1429 Senate St.
403 Rutledge Office Building
Columbia, SC 29201
803-734-8563
Fax: 803-734-8624

South Dakota
Adult Education
Office of Adult, Vocational and
   Technical Education
700 Governors Drive
Pierre, SD 57501-2291
605-773-4716
Fax: 605-773-6139

Tennessee
Executive Director
Division of Adult and Community
   Education
Department of Education
1130 Menzler Rd.
Nashville, TN 37210
615-741-7054
Fax: 615-741-6236

Texas
Program Director, Adult Education
Division of A.E./Employment
Training, Funding and Compliance
Texas Education Center
1701 North Congress Avenue
Austin, TX 78701
512-463-9294
Fax: 512-475-3575

Utah
Specialist
Adult Education Services
Office of Education
250 East 500 South St.
Salt Lake City, UT 84111
801-538-7844
Fax: 801-538-7521

Vermont
Chief, Adult Education Unit
Department of Education
State Office Building
Montpelier, VT 05602
802-828-3131
Fax: 802-828-3140

Virginia
Associate Director, A.E.
Department of Education
Commonwealth of Virginia
P.O. Box 6Q
Richmond, VA 23216
804-225-2075
Fax: 804-371-8593

Virgin Islands
Director, ABE
Department of Education
P.O. Box 6640
St. Thomas, VI 00801
809-774-5394
Fax: 809-774-4679

Washington
Director
Office of Adult Literacy
State Board for Community and
   Technical Colleges
P.O. Box 42495
Olympia, WA 98504-2495
206-664-9402
Fax: 206-664-8808

West Virginia
Assistant Director, A.E.
Department of Education
Building 6, Room 230
Capitol Complex
1900 Kanawha Blvd., East
Charleston, WV 25305
304-558-6318
Fax: 304-558-0048

Wisconsin
State Director, Vocational, Technical
   and Adult Education
Board of Vocational, Technical and
   Adult Education
310 Price Place
P.O. Box 7874
Madison, WI 53707
608-266-1207

Wyoming
Coordinator, Adult Education
Hathaway Building
Cheyenne, WY 82002
307-777-6228
Fax: 307-777-6234

Appendix B

State Employment Agencies

The state-by-state lists below will tell you what State Employment Agencies provide career counseling, vocational testing or other special services.

Alabama
Department of Industrial Relations
State Employment Service
649 Monroe Street
Montgomery, AL 36131
334-242-8003
Montgomery local office: 334-286-3700
> **Services:**
> Career/Vocational Counseling: Yes
> Testing: aptitude
> Other Services and Publications
> ✓ Labor market information
>
> ✓ Food Stamp Program: job training for individuals on food stamps
>
> ✓ Professional Placement Services: special counseling and help for white collar professionals

Alaska
Employment Security Division
Department of Labor
P.O. Box 25509
Juneau, AK 99802-5509
Juneau local office: 907-465-2711
>   **Services:**
>   Career/Vocational Counseling: yes
>   Testing: General aptitude, clerical, and self-interest
>   Other Services and Publications
>   ✓ Alaska Job Facts

Arizona
Department of Economic Security
DES Public Information Office
P.O. Box 6123
1717 W. Jefferson
Phoenix, AZ 85007
602-542-3667
>   **Services:**
>   Career/Vocational Counseling: yes
>   Testing: Aptitude
>   Other Services and Publications:
>   ✓ Food Stamp/ Job Search: refers eligible job seekers to Food Stamp program
>   ✓ Special summer employment compaigns
>   ✓ Work Incentive Demonstration Program (Workfare): helps AFDC recipients move toward economic self-support
>   ✓ Services Provided by DES

Arkansas
Employment Security Department
#2 Capitol Mall
Little Rock, AR 72203
501-682-2121
Local Little Rock office: 501-682-2127
Services:
Career/Vocational Counseling: only that involving Job Training
Partnership Act participants
Testing: yes, aptitude and clerical
Other services and Publications:
- ✓ Labor market information

- ✓ Employer Services: A Good Return on Your Investment; programs that companies use to get the employees they need.

California
Employment Development Department
800 Capitol Mall, Room 5000
Sacramento, CA 95814
916-653-0707
Local Sacramento office: 916-227-0300
Services:
Career/Vocational Counseling: Yes
Testing: Aptitude and clerical
Other Services and Publications:
- ✓ Job Search Workshops

- ✓ Labor market information and statistics

- ✓ Experience Unlimited program—helps unemployed managers, professionals and technical workers get back to work

- ✓ Job Match—computerized service that matches job applicant's skills with state-wide listing of job openings.

Colorado
Department of Labor and Employment
Division of Employment and Training
639 E. 18th Avenue
Denver, CO 80203
303-830-3011

Services:
Career/Vocational Counseling: Yes
Testing: Aptitude
Other Services and Publications:

✓ Labor market information

✓ Job Search Workshops-subjects include interviewing, writing resumes and where to look for jobs.

✓ Forty Plus of Colorado, Inc.—organizations of unemployed people 40 years of age or older who have professional or management experience and who help each other with job search.

✓ Summer Job Hunt—helps kids ages 16 through 21 find summer jobs.

✓ Year-round Youth Program—kids receive job placement help.

✓ Stay In School Campaign—kids who need money to stay in school can get certified to work part-time in the summer for the federal government.

Connecticut

Connecticut Department of Labor
Program Support
200 Folly Brook Blvd.
Wethersfield, CT 06109-1114
203-566-5160
Hartford local office: 203-566-5771

Services:
Career/Vocational Counseling: Yes
Testing: Clerical, Aptitude, Interest
Other Services and Publications:

✓ Shared Work Program: part-time employment along with proportional unemployment benefits

✓ Job Connection: businesses get tax credit for providing on-the-job training.

✓ Customized Job Training: group of workers are trained for a specific business's needs.

✓ Subsidized Transitional Employment Program: companies get wage subsidies as an incentive to hire certain workers.

✓ Employment Search Program: job help for mothers on welfare

✓ Labor market information.

Delaware

Department of Labor
Employment and Training Division
P.O. Box 9499
Newark, DE 19714-9499
302-761-8129
Newark local office: 302-368-6622

Services:
Career/Vocational Counseling: Yes
Testing: Aptitude
Other Services and Publications

✓ Directory of Job Training, Employment & Education Programs: includes listing of organizations and agencies in DE that offer job training programs.

✓ Women's Vocational Services: special employment and training services for divorced or separated women.

District of Columbia
Office of Job Service
Department of Employer Services
500 C St., NW, Room 317
Washington, DC 20001
202-724-7049

Services:
Career/Vocational Counseling: Yes
Testing: Clerical and Aptitude
Other Services and Publications:

✓ First Source Agreement Program: certain D.C. contractors must give job preference to D.C. residents

✓ Regional Employment Program: matches D.C. workers with job openings in the MD and VA suburbs

✓ A Real Chance: job opportunities for public assistance recipients

✓ Adult Literacy programs

✓ On-the-job training companies receive financial incentives to provide workers with on-the-job training.

✓ Training and Retraining for Employment Program: referrals, job placement, training, and allowances for those needing training.

Florida
Department of Labor and Employment Security
1320 Executive Center Dr.
300 Atkins Building
Tallahassee, FL 32301
904-488-7228

Services:
Career/Vocational Counseling: Yes, including workshops
Testing: Clerical and Aptitude
Other Services and Publications:

✓ Professional Placement Network: helps unemployed professionals find work through networking.

✓ Job Club: activities include resume writing, interviewing techniques, and more

✓ Job Skills Workshop

Georgia
Employment Services Division
Department of Labor
148 International Blvd.
Atlanta, GA 30303
404-656-6380
Atlanta local office: 404-699-6900

Services:

Career/Vocational Counseling: No

Testing: Clerical

Other Services and Publications:

✓ (Re)Place Yourself: A Job Hunting Guide

✓ Personal Data Book: A Record for Job Hunters

✓ Job Corps Services: screening for applicants

✓ OLIVOR System: a computerized system for unemployment benefits.

Hawaii
Hawaii State Employment Service
830 Punch Bowl St., Room 112
Honolulu, HI 96813
808-586-8700

Services:

Career/Vocational Counseling: On a very limited basis as time permits for general applicant. Do provide Veterans counseling.

Testing: No

For JTPA contact: Work Hawaii Brochure, 715 South King St., Suite 500, Honolulu, Hawaii 96813, 808-523-4221.

✓ Referral to job training programs

✓ Improving your English—referrals to free English improvement programs

✓ Child care and transportation—will help you with free transportation or child care if you need it while job searching.

✓ Disabled Veterans Outreach Program—helps veterans directly in their job search.

Idaho

Idaho Department of Employment
317 Main Street
Boise, ID 83735
208-334-6100
Boise local office: 208-334-6211
Services:
Career/Vocational Counseling: Yes
Testing: Clerical and Aptitude
Other Services and Publications:
✓ Rent-A-Kid Program: Job Service calls daily on kids to fill positions for employers.

✓ Wage Surveys for irrigators

Illinois

Department of Employment Security
401 S. State Street
Chicago, IL 60605
312-793-5700
Aurora local Job Service office: 708-844-6640
Services:
Career/Vocational Counseling: Yes, with emphasis on Vets
Testing: Clerical and Job Skills Aptitude
Other Services and Publications:
✓ Hire The Future: summer job program for teens

✓ Job Search computer system: matches applicants with job openings.

✓ Job Search Workshops

✓ Doorways to Jobs: A Directory of Job Training

✓ Illinois Department of Employment Security Services

✓ Merchandising Your Job Talents.

Indiana
Department of Workforce Development
10 N. Senate
Indianapolis, IN 46204
317-232-7670
Local Indianapolis office: 317-6842400
    Services:
    Career/Vocational Counseling: Yes, through workshops
    Testing: Yes, guidance testing and referral
    Other Services and Publications:
    ✓ Basic Education Classes

    ✓ Training Opportunities Workshops

    ✓ On-the-Job Training

    ✓ Academic Skills Upgrades: conducts classes for companies whose workers need to be better educated.

    ✓ Industry-Based Training: pays companies to retrain workers in-house.

    ✓ Labor market information

Iowa
Job Service Program Bureau
Department of Employment Services
1000 East Grand Avenue
Des Moines, IA 50319
800-562-4692
Des Moines local office: 512-281-9619
    Services:
    Career/Vocational Counseling: Yes
    Testing: Clerical

Kansas
Division of Employment and Training
Department of Human Resources
401 Topeka Avenue
913-296-5317
> **Services:**
> Career/Vocational Counseling: Yes
> Testing: Aptitude, Clerical
> Other Services and Publications:
> ✓ Job Search Workshops
> ✓ Chamber of Commerce relocation package: 913-234-2644
> ✓ Career Assistance Network: 913-273-5190
> ✓ Topeka Youth Project: 913-273-4141

Kentucky
Department of Employment Services
275 East Main Street, 2nd Floor
Frankfort, KY 40621
502-564-5331
Local Office: 502-564-7046 (Frankfort)
> **Services:**
> Career/Vocational Counseling: Yes
> Testing: Occupational, Clerical, Aptitude, Toyota Motor Corporation Skills Testing
> Other Services and Publications:
> ✓ On-the-job training
> ✓ JOBS: Job training and placement program for AFDC recipients.
> ✓ Professional Placement Network: help for management-level professionals who have lost their jobs—502-564-3906.

Louisiana
Office of Employment Security
Department of Labor
P.O. Box 94094
Baton Rouge, LA 70804-9094
504-342-3013
Local Baton Rouge office: 504-925-4311
Services:
Career/Vocational Counseling: No
Testing: Aptitude, Clerical
Other Services and Publications:
- ✓ Labor Market Information

- ✓ On-the-job Training

- ✓ Shared Work Unemployment Compensation: workers can work part-time and still earn a proportion of the unemployment insurance.

Maine
Job Service Division
Bureau of Employment Security
P.O. Box 309
Augusta, ME 04330
207-287-3431
Local Augusta office: 207-624-5120
Services:
Career/Vocational Counseling: Yes
Testing: General Aptitude
Other Services and Publications:
- ✓ Strategic Training for Accelerated Reemployment Program: help for those on unemployment get the help and training they need.

- ✓ Health Occupations Training Project: education and training in health care jobs.

- ✓ Jobs for Maine's Graduates Program: helps high school students make transition from school to job market.

- ✓ Maine Training Initiative Program: job training for those who don't qualify for JTPA job training.

- ✓ Summer Youth Program: provides work and basic education for teens during the summer.

- ✓ Resume Preparation Assistance.

Maryland
Job Service
Department of Employment and Economic Development
1100 North Eutaw St., Room 208
Baltimore, MD 21201
410-767-2000
Local Baltimore office: 410-767-2121
   Services:
   Career/Vocational Testing: Yes
   Testing: Clerical, Aptitude
   Other Services and Publications:
   ✓ On-the-job Training
   ✓ Courses offered at local community college
   ✓ Area skill development centers

Massachusetts
Department of Employment and Training
19 Staniford Street
Boston, MA 02114
617-626-6000
Boston local office: 617-626-6000
   Services:
   Career/Vocational counseling Yes, job specialists available
   Testing: Clerical, Aptitude
   Other Services and Publications:
   ✓ Training and Employment Directory: listing of jobs and places to
     get the necessary training for them in the state.
   ✓ Personal employment plan: creates a special job plant to your needs.
   ✓ Resume writing services
   ✓ Job search workshops

   Use of:
   ✓ Fax machines
   ✓ Photocopiers
   ✓ Telephones
   ✓ Job guides
   ✓ Labor market books
   ✓ Career resource materials
   ✓ Child care listings
   ✓ Transportation information

Michigan
Bureau of Employment Service
Employment Security Commission
7310 Woodward Ave.
Detroit, MI 48202
313-876-5309
Local Detroit office: 313-822-9510
Services:
Career/Vocational Counseling: Yes
Testing: Aptitude, Clerical, Interest Inventory
Other Services and Publications:
✓ Labor market data
✓ Local statewide, and interstate job banks
✓ Job service resume system
✓ Job development
✓ Job seeking skills workshops and Job Clubs
✓ Occupational information

Minnesota
Reemployment Program
Administration
390 N. Roberts St.
St. Paul, MN 55101
612-297-2177
Local St. Paul office: 612-642-0363
Services:
Career/Vocational Counseling: Yes, to those facing employment barriers
Testing: Proficiency and aptitude as well as vocational
Other Services and Publications:
✓ Mass recruitment: screening for companies needing large numbers of workers.
✓ Referral to community-based agencies

Mississippi
Mississippi Employment Security Commission
1520 West Capitol Street
P.O. Box 1699
Jackson, MS 39215-1699
601-961-7478
601-354-8711
Southfort local office: 601-961-7802
   Services:
   Career/Vocational Counseling: Yes
   Testing: Yes, Clerical, Aptitude (not all offices)
   Other Services and Publications:
   ✓ Labor market Information

Missouri
Employment Services
Division of Employment Security (DOLIR)
P.O. Box 59
Jefferson City, MO 65104
314-751-3976
Jefferson local office: 314-526-8115
   Services:
   Career/Vocational Counseling: Yes
   Testing: Clerical, when requested by employer
   Other Services and Publications:
   ✓ Automated job match: your skills, abilities and salary require-
     ments are matched up with available job openings.
   ✓ Missouri Resume Retrieval Service: when job opening occurs,
     your resume automatically sent to employer.
   ✓ Labor Market Information.

Montana
Job Service/Employment and Training Division
P.O. Box 1728
Helena, MT 59624
406-444-4100
Helena local office: 406-447-3200
Services:
Career/Vocational Counseling: Yes
Testing: Aptitude, Clerical, Literacy, Interest
Other Services and Publications:
- ✓ Teacher Placement: special program that matches up teachers and school administrators with available job openings in MT.
- ✓ On-the-job training: businesses received subsidy to provide workers with on-the-job training.
- ✓ For A Working Montana: outlines all the job programs
- ✓ Job matching system
- ✓ Labor market information

Nebraska
Job Training Program
Department of Labor
P.O. Box 94600
Lincoln, NE 68509
402-471-2127
Lincoln local office: 402-441-7111
Services:
Career/Vocational Counseling: Yes
Testing: Aptitude
Other Services and Publications:
- ✓ Work Experience: a paid employment experience with a public or non-profit agency.
- ✓ Classroom training: available through community colleges.
- ✓ Pacific Institute: develops independent thinking skills to set personal and professional goals.
- ✓ On-the-Job training.

Nevada
Department of Employment, Training, and Rehabilitation
Employment Security Division
500 East Third Street
Carson City, NV 89713
702-687-4650
Carson City local office: 702-687-4560
>   **Services:**
>   Vocational/Career Counseling: Yes
>   Testing: Aptitude, Performance, Interest
>   Other Services and Publications:
>   - ✓ On-the-job Training
>   - ✓ Claimant Employment Program: helps put workers claiming unemployment into job training programs.
>   - ✓ Job Search Skills Workshops: resume preparation, interviewing skills, and appropriate dress.
>   - ✓ Short-term Labor: provides part-time work for those eligible to work at a moment's notice.
>   - ✓ Employment Guide: Nevada Job Finding Techniques.

New Hampshire
Employment Service Bureau
Department of Employment Security
32 South Main Street
Concord, NH 03301
603-224-3311
Local Concord Office: 603-228-4100
>   **Services:**
>   Vocational/Career Counseling: Yes
>   Testing: Aptitude, Performance, Interest
>   Other Services and Publications:
>   - ✓ Outstanding Personnel List: local employment offices select job seekers who have high levels of achievement to show employers.
>   - ✓ Community Work Experience Program: gain work experience through community organizations.
>   - ✓ On-the-job training.
>   - ✓ Referral to supportive services.
>   - ✓ How to Prepare Yourself for Job Interviews
>   - ✓ Veterans Resource Directory
>   - ✓ Job Interviewing Techniques

New Jersey
Employment Services
New Jersey Department of Labor
Labor and Industry Bldg., CN 058
Trenton, NJ 08625
609-292-5005
Local Office: 609-292-0620
   Services:
   Career/Vocational Counseling: Yes
   Testing: GATB, Uses Interest Inventory
   ✓ Vocational Information Profile (VIP)

   Other Services and Publications:
   ✓ Career evaluation

   ✓ Training programs for newly locating companies: companies new to an area and looking for skilled workers may qualify for free training.

   ✓ Job Development

   ✓ World of Work seminars

   ✓ Job Hunters Guide

New Mexico
New Mexico Department of Labor
P.O. Box 1928
Albuquerque, NM 87103
505-841-8406
Local Office: 505-841-9327
   Services:
   Career/Vocational Counseling
   Testing: Clerical, Aptitude
   Other Services and Publications:
   ✓ Career Information System: computer program that tells you what you need to do given your background and career goals.

   ✓ Large Employers in the Albuquerque Area

127

New York

New York State Department of Labor
Community Service Division
State Campus
Building 12, Room 582
Albany, NY 12240
518-457-3584
Local Office: 518-465-0797
  Services:
  Career/Vocational Counseling: Yes
  Testing: Aptitude, clerical, literacy and career interest
  Other Services and Publications:
  - ✓ On-the-job training: screen workers for available opportunities to train on the job.

  - ✓ Displaced Homemaker Program: provides counseling, training, support services and job placement to homemakers who have lost their support.

  - ✓ Job Search Skills: tip sheets, workshops, and siminars

  - ✓ Project Trabago: makes sure job programs are accessible to Hispanic community; provides needed translation help.

  - ✓ Rural Programs: offer help to seasonal farm workers find jobs.

  - ✓ Community services: referral to appropriate human service programs for the unemployed.

  - ✓ Benefits for Veterans and Their Families.

North Carolina

Employment Security Commission
P.O. Box 27625
Raleigh, NC 27611
919-733-7522
Local office: 919-733-3941
  Services:
  Vocational/Career Counseling: Yes
  Testing: Aptitude, Clerical

North Dakota
Employment and Training Division
Job Service
P.O. Box 5507
Bismarck, ND 58502
701-328-2861
Loval Job Service: 701-328-5000
   Services:
   Vocational/Career Counseling: Yes
   Testing: Aptitude and Interest, Typing and Spelling
   Other Services and Publications:
   ✓ Job Search Assistance workshops
   ✓ JOBS

Ohio
Ohio Employment Service Division
Ohio Bureau of Employment Services
145 South Front Street
Columbus, OH 43215
614-466-4636
Local office: 614-268-7990 (North)
614-237-2585 (East)
   Services:
   Vocational/Career Counseling: Yes
   Testing: Clerical, Aptitude
   Other Services and Publications:
   ✓ Child care information: provides a computer printout of licensed
      day care centers in your area.
   ✓ Ex-offender services
   ✓ Writing an Effective Resume
   ✓ Job Search Techniques
   ✓ Ohio Military Transition Assistance Program
   ✓ Job Search Strategies

Oklahoma
Oklahoma Employment Service
Employment Security Commission
Will Rogers Memorial Office Building
2401 North Lincoln Blvd.
Oklahoma City, OK 73105
405-557-0200
Local office: 405-424-0881
  Services:
  Vocational/Career Counseling: Yes
  Testing: Spelling, Typing and Dictation
  Other Services and Publications:
  ✓ Labor market information
  ✓ Job Development: Service contacts employer on behalf of job applicant with specific skills where no job openings in the local office for that particular skill.
  ✓ Computerized Matching: job seekers are matched with job openings.

Oregon
Oregon Employment Department
875 Union Street, NE
Salem, OR 97311
503-378-8420
Local Office: 503-378-4846
  Services:
  Vocational/Career Counseling: only through the JTPA program
  Testing: Clerical (nonaptitude available)
  Other Services and Publications:
  ✓ Timber Industry Dislocated Workers Program

Pennsylvania
Bureau of Job Center Field Operations
Labor and Industry Building, Room 419
Seventh and Forster Streets
Harrisburg, PA 17121
717-787-3354
Local Office: 717-783-3270
Services:
Vocational/Career Counseling: Yes
Testing: Skills Testing: Aptitude (when requested by employer)
Other Services and Publications:
Pennsylvania Conservation Corps: summer and year-round work on public
land and in community centers for young people, ages 14 to 25.
- ✓ On-the-Job Training
- ✓ Career Guide Newspaper

Rhode Island
Department of Employment and Training
101 Friendship Street
Providence, RI 02903
401-277-3732
Local Office: 401-277-3606
Services:
Vocational/Career Counseling: Yes
Testing: GATB, CDM (Career Decision Maker) and APTICOM,
as well as clerical
Other Services and Publications:
- ✓ Job Search Workshops: covers interviewing, applications, and
  marketing job skills
- ✓ Resume Writing Seminars: professionally printed resumes pro-
  vided to help you with job search.
- ✓ Call-A-Teen Program: a statewide, odd job employment pro-
  grams for teens 14 to 17 years old.
- ✓ Tuition Waivers: for courses at state colleges or universities if
  you're receiving benefits.

South Carolina
South Carolina Employment Service
P.O. Box 995
Columbia, SC 29202
803-737-2400
Local Office: 803-737-9935
Services:
Vocational/Career Counseling: Yes
Testing: Clerical, at employers request, aptitude
Other Services and Publications:
✓ Rural manpower service programs: help seasonal farmworkers with referrals to employment agencies and support services.

✓ South Carolina Employer Services Catalog.

South Dakota
South Dakota Department of Labor
700 Governors Drive
Pierre, SD 57501
605-773-3101
Local Office: 605-773-3372
Services:
Vocational/Career Counseling: yes
Testing: yes, clerical aptitude
Other Services and Publications:
✓ Job Related Education: job specific education that furthers the training in your chosen field.

✓ Skill Training: training conducted for up to two years at vocational schools and college.

✓ Work Experience program: pays you federal minimum wage while you work at a real job.

✓ How Job Service Can Help You Find A Job

✓ How Job Training Can Improve Your Work Skills

Tennessee
Department of Employment Security
Volunteer Plaza, 12th Floor
500 James Robertson Parkway
Nashville, TN 37243
615-741-2131
Local Office: 615-741-3626
   Services:
   Vocational/Career Counseling: yes
   Testing: Aptitude
   Other Services and Publications:
   ✓ Referral to skill training

Texas
Texas Employment Commission
101 East 15th Street
Austin, TX 78778
512-463-2222
Local Office: 512-478-8734
Information: 512-463-2873
   Services:
   Other Services and Publications:
   ✓ Annual Report of the Texas Employment Commission

Utah
Job Service
Department of Employment Security
Administration
140 East, 300 South
Salt Lake City, UT 84101
801-536-7400
Public Relations: 801-536-7462
Local Office: 801-536-7000
   Services:
   Vocational/Career Counseling: yes
   Testing: GATB, Proficiency (typing, dictation, spelling)
   Other Services and Publications:
   ✓ Temporary Placement Offices in Salt Lake and Ogden
   ✓ Job Seeking Skills Workshop
   ✓ Labor market information

Vermont
Employment Service Administration
Department of Employment and Training
P.O. Box 488
Montpelier, VT 05602
802-229-0311
Local Office: 802-828-3860
> **Services:**
> Vocational/Career Counseling: yes
> Testing: GATB, Interest Inventory Profile (VIP), Basic Skills assessments
> Other Services and Publications:
> - ✓ Group Assessment (COMPASS): help in focusing on career choices.
> - ✓ Vermont Occupational Information System: information on job projections, job specific education.
> - ✓ Federal Occupational and Career Information System: matches your interests and abilities with suitable Federal jobs.
> - ✓ State Training Inventory: a computer file of training programs being offered at schools and training institutions in the northeast.

Virginia
Virginia Employment Commissioner
703 East Main Street
Richmond, VA 23219
804-786-3001
Local office: 804-674-3650
> **Services:**
> Career/Vocational Counseling: yes
> Testing: Typing, if required by job order
> Other Services and Publications:
> - ✓ JOBS program: offers education, training, and job-related services to welfare recipients.
> - ✓ Federal Contractor Job Listing: companies with large federal government contracts lists jobs with VA Job Service.
> - ✓ Labor market information
> - ✓ Employability training

Washington
Washington Employment Security Department
TRB 2 Unit
P.O. Box 9046
Olympia, WA 98507-9046
360-753-0747
Local Office: 206-438-7800
Services:
Career/Vocational Counseling: yes
Testing: Not on a regular basis, although will do some aptitude testing for specific individuals with need
Other Services and Publications:
✓ JobNet: matches workers' skills and abilities with available jobs in any geographical area.

✓ Classroom, vocational and on-the-job training

✓ Job Search Workshops: resume writing, interviewing techniques, grooming and more.

✓ Job Search Skills Training Program: special retraining program for workers who have been injured on the job.

✓ Special Employment Services (Dislocated Timber Workers): screens unemployed timber workers who are eligible to receive four days of work and one day of training per week.

West Virginia
West Virginia Bureau of Employment Programs
112 California Ave.
Charleston, WV 25305-0112
304-558-2630
Local Office: 304-558-0342
Services:
Career/Vocational Counseling: yes
Testing: Aptitude and proficiency tests
Other Services and Publications:

Wisconsin
Department of DILHR
Job Service, 2nd Florr
201 East Washington Ave.
Madison, WI 53702
608266-0327 Department of Job Service
Local office: 608-266-1492
Services:
Vocational/Career counseling: Yes
Testing: Typing, general aptitude (for apprenticeships only)
Other Services and Publications:
- ✓ Setting Employment Goals
- ✓ Interviewing Skills/Techniques
- ✓ Resume and Job Search Assistance

Wyoming
Wyoming Department of Employment
P.O. Box 2760
Casper, WY 82602
307-235-3611
Services:
Career/Vocational Counseling: Yes
Testing and Assessment Services: Yes
Other Services:
- ✓ Computerized listing of job openings
- ✓ On-the-job training
- ✓ Labor market information
- ✓ Resume preparation assistance
- ✓ Workshops
- ✓ Resource center

Appendix C

U.S. Office of Personnel Management

Federal Employment Information Centers

Alabama
520 Wynn Drive N.W.
Huntsville, AL 35818-3426
205-837-0894

Alaska
222 West 7th Ave., #22 Room 158
Anchorage, AK 99513-7522
907-271-5821

Arizona
(See New Mexico)

California
9650 Flair Dr., Suite 100A
El Monte, CA 91731
818-575-6510

1029 J St., Room 202
Sacramento, CA 95814
416-744-5627

Federal Building, Room 4260
880 Front Street
San Diego, CA 92101
818-575-8510

120 Howard Street, Suite B
San Francisco, CA 94120
415-744-5627

Colorado
12345 W. Alameda Parkway
Lakewood, CO 60225
303-969-7050

Connecticut
(See Boston, Massachusetts)

Delaware
(See Philadelphia, Pennsylvania)

District of Columbia
Theodore Roosevelt Federal Building
1900 E St., NW, Room 1416
Washington, DC 20415
202-606-2700

Florida
Claude Pepper Federal Building,
    Room 1222
61 SW First Avenue
Miami, FL (walk in only)

Commodore Building, Suite 125
3444 McCrory Place
Orlando, FL (walk in only)

Georgia
Richard B. Russell Building, Room
940A
75 Spring Street, SW
Atlanta, GA 30303
404-331-4315

Hawaii
Federal Building, Room 5316
300 Alamoana Blvd.
Honolulu, HI 96850
808-541-2791

Idaho
(See Seattle, Washington)

Illinois
230 South Dearborn St., Room 2916
Chicago, IL 60804
312-353-6192

Indiana
(See Michigan)

Iowa
(See Kansas City, Missouri)
816-426-7820

Kentucky
(See Ohio)

Louisiana
1515 Poydras St., Suite 608
New Orleans, LA 70112
210-805-2402

Maine
(See Philadelphia, Pennsylvania)

Massachusetts
10 Causeway Street
Boston, MA 02222
617-565-5900

Michigan
477 Michigan Avenue, Room 565
Detroit, MI 48228
313-226-6950

Minnesota
Bishop Henry Whipple Federal Bldg.
1 Federal Drive, Room 501
Fort Snelling, MN 55111
612-725-3430

Mississippi
(See Alabama)

Missouri
Federal Building, Room 134
601 E. 12th Street
Kansas City, MO 64106
816-426-5702

400 Old Post Office Building
815 Olive Street
St. Louis, MO 63101
314-539-2285

Montana
(See Colorado)

Nebraska
(See Kansas City)
816-426-7819

Nevada
(for Clark, Lincoln, and Nye
counties, see
Los Angeles, California: all other
counties
See Sacramento, California)

New Hampshire
(See Boston, Massachusetts)

New Jersey
(See New York City, New York
or Philadelphia, Pennsylvania)

New Mexico
605 Marquette Avenue, Suite 910
Albuquerque, NM 87102
505-766-5583

New York
Jacob K. Javits Building
Second Floor, Room 120
26 Federal Plaza
New York City, NY 10278
212-264-0422

P.O. Box 7267
100 South Clinton Street
Syracuse, NY 13261
315-448-0480

North Carolina
4407 Bland Road, Suite 202
Raleigh, NC 27609
919-790-2822

North Dakota
(See Minnesota)

Ohio
Federal Building, Room 506
200 W. 2nd Street
Dayton, OH 45402
513-225-2720

Oklahoma
(See San Antonio, Texas)

Oregon
Federal Building, Room 376
1220 SW Third Ave.
Portland, OR 97204
503-326-3141

Pennsylvania
Federal Building, Room 168
P.O. Box 761
Harrisburg, PA 17108
717-782-4494

William J. Green, Jr. Federal Building
600 Arch Street
Philadelphia, PA 19106
215-597-7440

Federal Building
1000 Liberty Ave., Room 119
Pittsburgh, PA 15222
(See Philadelphia for telephone)

Puerto Rico
U.S. Federal Building, Room 328
150 Carlos Chardon Avenue
San Juan, PR 00918
609-766-5242

Rhode Island
(See Boston, Massachusetts)

South Carolina
(See Raleigh, North Carolina)

South Dakota
(See Minnesota)

Tennessee
(See Alabama)

Texas
(Corpus Christi: see San Antonio)
512-884-8113

Dallas
(See San Antonio)

Harlingen
(See San Antonio)
512-769-0455

8610 Broadway, Room 305
San Antonio, TX 78217
210-805-2402

Utah
(See Colorado)

Vermont
(See Puerto Rico)
809-774-8790

Virginia
Federal Building, Room 500
200 Granby Street
Norfolk, VA 23510
804-441-3335

Washington
Federal Building, Room 110
915 Second Avenue
Seattle, WA 98174
206-220-6400

Washington, DC
(See District of Columbia)

West Virginia
(See Ohio)
513-225-2866

Wisonsin
(for Dane, Grant, Green, Iowa,
   Lafayette,
Jefferson, Walworth, Milwaukee,
   Racine,
Waukkesha, Rock and Kenosha, see
Illinois listing. 312-353-6189; for all
Other counties see Minnesota,
   612-725-3430)

Wyoming
(See Colorado)

Appendix D

State Government Jobs

Be certain to complete in detail the job application and file it with the designated before the deadline date. If you are a veteran you will undoubtedly get a preference. Also note whether a written examination is required for the job.

Alabama
State Personnel Department
300 State Administration Building
64 North Union Street
Montgomery, AL 36130
334-242-3389

Alaska
Alaska Division of Personnel
Department of Administration
P.O. Box 110201
Juneau, AK 99811-0201
907-465-4430
Job Bank: 907-465-8910
www.state.ak.us

Arizona
Arizona State Personnel Division
Department of Administration
1831 W. Jefferson
Phoenix, AZ 85007
602-542-5482
Job Bank: 602-542-4966
www.state.az.us

Arkansas
Office of Personnel Management
Department of Finance and
    Administration
1509 W. 7th St., Room 201
Little Rock, AR 72201
501-682-1823
Job Bank: 501-682-5627
www.state.ar.us

California
California State Personnel
P.O. Box 944201
Sacramento, CA 94244-2010
916-653-1705
Los Angeles: 213-620-6450
San Diego: 619-237-6163
San Francisco: 415-557-7871
TDD: 916-445-2689
Job Bank: 916-445-0538
www.ca.gov

...orado

...te Dept. of Human Resources
1313 Sherman Street, Room 110
Denver, CO 80203
303-866-2321
www.state.co.us

Connecticut

State Resource and Employment Center
165 Capitol Avenue
Hartford, CT 06106
203-566-2501
www.state.ct.us

Delaware

State Personnel Office
First Street Plaza, 3rd Floor
Wilmington, DE 19801
302-739-4195
www.state.de.us

District of Columbia

D.C. Personnel Department
441 4th Street, NW
Washington, DC 20001
202-727-6099
www.dchomepage.net

Florida

State Personnel Department
Room 1902
The Capitol
Tallahassee, FL 32399-0250
904-488-1176
Job Bank: 904-488-1179
Fax: 904-922-4928
www.state.fl.us

Georgia

Merit System of Personnel Admin.
West Tower, Suite 418
200 Piedmont Avenue
Atlanta, GA 30334
404-656-2705
Job Bank: 404-656-2725
Fax: 404-656-9740

Hawaii

Hawaii Department of Personnel
235 South Beretania Street, 11th Fl.
Honolulu, HA 96813-2437
808-587-0977
Job Bank: 808-587-0977
Fax: 808-587-1003
www.state.hawaii.gov

Idaho

State Personnel Commission
P.O. Box 83720
Boise, ID 83720-0066
208-334-2263
800-554-JOBS
Job Bank: 208-334-2568
Fax: 208-334-3182
www.state.id.us

Illinois

Bureau of Personnel Department of
 Management Services
503 Stratton Office Building
Springfield, IL 62706
217-782-6179
Fax: 217-524-8740
www.state.il.us

Indiana

Indiana Department of Personnel
402 West Washington St.
Indiana Government Center South
Indianapolis, IN 46204-2261
317-232-3105
Fax: 317-233-0236
www.state.in.us./acin/personnel

Iowa

Iowa Department of Personnel
Grimes State Office Building
East 14th and Grand
Des Moines, IA 50319
515-281-3351
Fax: 515-242-6450
Job Bank: 515-281-5820
www.state.ia.us/jobs/index.htm

Kansas

Kansas Division of Personnel Services
Department of Administration
Room 951, South Landon Building
Topeka, KS 66612
913-296-5390
www.state.ks.us

Kentucky

Kentucky Department of Personnel
200 Fair Oaks Lane, Suite 517
Frankfort, KY 40601
502-564-4460
www.state.ky.us

Louisiana

Louisiana Civil Service Commission
Division of Personnel
P.O. box 94111
Baton Rouge, LA 70804-9111
504-342-8536
Fax: 504-342-2386
www.state.la.us

Maine

Human Resources Department
4 Statehouse
Augusta, ME 04333
207-287-3761
www.state.me.us

Maryland

Maryland Department of Personnel
301 West Preston Street
Baltimore, MD 21201
410-225-4851
Fax: 410-333-5764
http://dop.state.md.us

Massachusetts

Division of Personnel Administration
1 Ashburton Place
Boston, MA 02108
617-727-3777
Fax: 617-727-3970
www.magnet.state.ma.us

Michigan

Michigan Department of Civil
  Services
400 South Pine
P.O. Box 30002
Lansing, MI 48909
517-373-2819
Fax: 517-373-7690

Minnesota

Minnesota Department of Employee
  Relations
200 Centennial Office Building
658 Cedar Street
St. Paul, MN 55155
612-296-8366
Fax: 612-296-8919
www.state.mn.us

Mississippi

Mississippi State Personnel Board
301 North Lamar Street, Suite 100
Jackson, MS 39201
601-359-2725
Fax: 601-359-2380
www.state.ms.us

Missouri

Missouri Division of Personnel
P.O. Box 388
Jefferson City, MO 65102
314-751-4162
Fax: 573-751-8641
www.state.mo.us

Montana

Montana Personnel Division
Mitchell Building, Room 130
Helena, MT 59620
406-444-3871
Fax: 406-447-3224
www.mt.gov

Nebraska
Nebraska Department of Personnel
301 Centennial Mall South
P.O. Box 94905
Lincoln, NE 68509
402-471-2075
Job Bank: 402-471-2200
Fax: 407-471-3754
www.state.ne.us

Nevada
Nevada Department of Personnel
209 East Musser St.
Carson City, NV 89710
702-687-4050
Job Bank: 702-687-4160

New Hampshire
New Hampshire Div. of Personnel
25 Capitol St., Room 1
Concord, NH 03301
603-271-3261
www.state.nh.us

New Jersey
New Jersey Department of Personnel
44 South Clinton Avenue, CN318
Trenton, NJ 08625
609-292-8668
Fax: 609-777-0905
www.state.nj.us

New Mexico
New Mexico State Personnel Office
P.O. Box 26127
Santa Fe, NM 87502-0127
www.state.nm.us

New York
New York State Personnel Board
Department of Civil Services
State Campus, Building #1
Albany, NY 12239
518-457-6216
518-457-3701
www.state.ny.us

North Carolina
North Carolina Office of State
   Personnel
116 West Jones St.
Raleigh, NC 27603
919-733-7922
Fax: 919-733-0653
www.state.nc.us

North Dakota
North Dakota Central Personnel
   Division
Office of Management and Budget
State Capitol
600 East Blvd., Avenue
Bismarck, ND 58505
701-328-3290
Fax: 701-328-5049
www.state.nd.us

Ohio
Ohio Division of Personnel
Division of Human Resources
30 East Broad St., 28th Floor
Columbus, OH 43215
614-466-4026
Job Bank: 614-466-4026
www.ohio.gov

Oklahoma
Office of Personnel Management
Jim Thorpe Building, Room 22
Oklahoma City, OK 73105
405-521-6337
Fax: 405-521-6308

Oregon
Oregon Personnel and Labor
   Relations Division
155 Cottage St., NE
Salem, OR 97310
503-378-5419
www.state.or.us

Pennsylvania
Pennsylvania State Employment
  Services
Office of Administration
110 Finance Building
Harrisburg, PA 17120
717-787-5703
www.state.pa.us

Rhode Island
Office of Personnel Administration
Department of Administration
One Capitol Hill
Providence, RI 02908
401-277-2172
Fax: 401-277-6391

South Carolina
South Carolina Human Resources
  Management Division
221 Divine St., 1st Floor
Columbus, SC 29250
803-734-9333
Fax: 803-734-9098
www.state.sc.us

South Dakota
South Dakota Office of Executive
  Management
Bureau of Personnel
500 East Capitol Avenue
Pierre, SD 57501
605-773-4918
Job Bank: 605-773-3326
Fax: 605-773-4344
www.state.sd.us

Tennessee
Tennessee Department of Personnel
James K. Polk Building, 2nd Floor
500 Deadrick Street
Nashville, TN 37243
615-741-4841
Fax: 615-741-6985
www.state.tn.us

Texas
Texas State Employment Commission
101 East 15th Street
Austin, TX 78778
512-463-1792
www.texas.gov

Utah
Utah Department of Human
  Resources Management
2120 State Office Building
Salt Lake City, UT 84114
801-538-3058
Job Bank: 801-538-3118
Fax: 801-538-3081
www.state.ut.us

Vermont
Vermont Department of Personnel
110 State Street
Montpelier, VT 05602
802-828-3483
Job Bank: 802-828-3483
Fax: 802-828-3409
www.vermont.state

Virginia
Virginia Department of Personnel
  and Training
James Monroe Building, 12th Floor
101 North 14th Street
Richmond, VA 23219
804-225-2131
Fax: 804-371-7401
www.state.va.us

Washington
Washington Department of Personnel
521 Capitol Way South
P.O. Box 47500
Olympia, WA 98504-7500
360-753-5358
Job Bank: 360-753-586-0545
www.wa.gov

West Virginia
West Virginia Division of Personnel
Capitol Complex Building, #6,
  Rm. 416
1900 Kanawha Blvd.
Charleston, WV 25305
304-558-5946
Fax: 304-558-1399
www.state.wv.us

Wisconsin
Wisconsin Department of
  Employment Relations
137 East Wilson Street
P.O. Box 7855
Madison, WI 53707-7855
608-266-9820
Job Bank: 608-266-1731
Fax: 608-267-1000
www.state.wi.us

Wyoming
Wyoming Personnel Division
Department of Administration and
  Information
2001 Capitol Av., Emerson Building
Cheyenne, WY 82002
307-777-6713
www.state.wy.us

Appendix E

Franchise Directories

Franchise Opportunities Handbook
By LaVerne L. Luddex, 1999
Jist Works, Inc.
720 North Park Avenue
Indianapolis, IN 46202-3490
800-648-JIST
800-JIST-FAX
Web Site www.jist.com

The Franchise Annual
Editor Ted Dixon
Info Press, Inc.
728 Center Street
P.O. Box 826
Lewiston, NY 14092
(716) 754-4669

The 200 Best Franchises To Buy
By Constance Jones
Bantam Books
1540 Broadway
New York, NY 10036

Directory of Franchising Organizations
1998/1999 Edition
Pilot Books
127 Sterling Avenue
Greenport, NY 11944

Appendix F

Small Business Administration

Field Offices and Phone Numbers

REGION I
40 Western Avenue, Room 512
Augusta, ME 04330
207-622-8378 ext. 101

Stewart Nelson Plaza
143 North Main Street, Suite 202
Concord, NH 03301
603-225-1400

87 State Street Room 205
Montpelier, VT 05602
802-828-4422

10 Causeway Street, Room 265
Boston, MA 0222-1093
617-565-5587

380 Westminister St., Room 511
Providence, RI 02903
401-528-4576
330 Main St., 2nd Floor
Hartford, CT 06106
860-240-4700

REGION II
Carlos Chardon Avenue, Room 691
Hato Rey, PR 00918
787-766-5422

26 Federal Plaza, Room 3100
New York, NY 10278
212-264-2454

401 South Salina, 5th Floor
Syracuse, NY 13260-2413
315-471-9393

111 West Huron Street Room 1311
Buffalo, NY 14202
716-551-5664

333 East Water Street, 4th Floor
Elmira, NY 14901
607-734-8130

35 Pinelawn Rd., Room 207W
Melville, NY 11747
516-454-0750

Two Gateway Center, 4th Floor
Neward, NJ 07102
973-645-6049

REGION III
10 S. Howard Street, Suite 6220
Baltimore, MD 21202
410-962-6195 ext. 337

1110 Vermont Avenue, 9th Floor
Washington, DC 20005
202-606-4000 ext. 259

409 3rd Street, SW, 7th Floor
Washington, DC 20416
202-205-6598

1824 Market Street, Suite 610
Wilmington, DE 19801
302-573-6294

168 W. Main Street, 6th Floor
Clarksburg, WV 26301
304-623-5631

405 Capital Street
Room 412
Charleston, WV 25301
304-347-5220

1504 Santa Rosa Road, Suite 200
Richmond, VA 23229
804-771-2400

Allendale Square
475 Allendale Road
King of Prussia, PA 19006
215-580-2706

Federal Building Liberty Avenue
Room 1120
Pittsburgh, PA 15222-4004
412-395-6560 ext. 223

20 North Penn Avenue
Wilkes-Barre, PA 18701
717-826-6197

100 Chestnut Street, Suite 108
Harrisburg, PA 17101
717-826-6197

REGION IV
7825 Baymeadows Way
Suite 100-B
Jacksonville, FL 32256-7504
904-443-1900

100 South Biscayne Blvd., 7th Floor
Miami, FL 33131
305-536-5521

188 Federal Office Building
600 Martin Luther King Place
Louisville, KY 40202
502-582-5971 ext. 239

50 Vantage Way, Suite 201
Nashville, TN 37228-1500
615-736-5881

200 North College Street, Room 300
Charlotte, NC 28202
704-344-6589 ext. 1124

1835 Assembly Street Room 358
Columbia, SC 29201
803-765-5377

1720 Peachtree St., NW
Suite 600
Atlanta, GA 30367
404-347-4749 ext. 108

2121 8th Avenue North, Suite 200
Birmingham, AL 35203-2398
205-731-1344

First Jackson Center
101 West Capitol St., Suite 400
Jackson, MS 39269
601-965-4378

BancorpSouth Plaza
2909 13th Street, Suite 203
Gulfport, MS 39501-1949
228-863-4627

REGION V
100 North 6th St., 610c Butler
    Square
Minneapolis, MN 55403
612-370-2322

212 East Washington Avenue
Room 213
Madison, WI 53703
608-264-5542

Henry Russ Federal Plaza
310 West Wisconsin Ave., Suite 400
Milwaukee, WI 53203
414-297-1231

477 Michigan Avenue, Room 515
Detroit, MI 48226
313-226-6075

228 W. Capital Avenue, Suite 11
Marquette, MI 49855
906-225-1108

500 W. Madison St., Room 1250
Chicago, IL 60661
312-353-5429

511 West Capitol Street, 3rd Floor
Illinois Financial Center
Springfield, IL 62701
906-225-1108

429 N. Pennsylvania Street, Suite 100
Indianapolis, IN 46204-1873
317-226-7272 ext. 240

2 Nationwide Plaza, Suite 1400
Columbus, OH 43215-2542
614-469-6860

525 Vine Street, Suite 870
Cincinnati, OH 45202
513-684-2814

REGION VI
365 Canal Street, Suite 2250
New Orleans, LA 70130
504-589-2706

2120 River Front Drive #100
Little Rock, AR 72201-1747
501-324-5874 ext. 239

210 Park Avenue, Suite 130
Harlingen, TX 78550
956-427-8533

9301 Southwest Freeway, Suite 550
Houston, TX 77054-1591
713-773-6500

1611 Tenth Street, Suite 200
Lubbock, TX 79401
806-472-7462 ext. 248

727 E. Durango Blvd., Room A-527
San Antonio, TX 78206-1204
210-472-5928

10737 Gateway West, Suite 320
El Paso, TX 79935
915-540-5564

4300 Amon Carter Blvd., Suite 114
Ft. Worth, TX 76155
817-885-6500

625 Silver SW, Suite 320
Albuquerque, NM 87102
505-346-6752

REGION VII
11145 Mill Valley Road
Omaha, NE 68154
402-221-7208

210 Walnut Street Room 749
Des Moines, IA 50309
515-284-4653

215 4th Avenue, SE
Suite 200
Cedar Rapids, IA 52401-1806
319-362-6405 ext. 218

100 East English, Suite 510
Wichita, KS 67202
316-269-6273

323 W. 8th Street, Suite 501
Kansas City, MO 64105
816-374-6701 ext. 238

815 Olive Street, Room 242
St. Louis, MO 63101
314-539-6600 ext. 252

620 S. Glenston St., Suite 110
Springfield, MO 65802-3200
417-864-7670 ext. 125

REGION VIII
301 South Park, Room 528
Helena, MT 59626
406-446-1081 ext. 138

100 East B. St.
P.O. Box 2839
Casper, WY 82602
307-261-6500

657 2nd Avenue, Room 219
Fargo, ND 58108
701-239-5131 ext. 207

1st Financial Center, Suite 1200
Sioux Falls, SD 57104-727
605-330-4231

125 South State Street, Room 2237
Salt Lake City, UT 84138
801-524-5804

721 19th Street, P.O. Box 660
Denver, CO 80202
303-844-3461

REGION IX
455 Market Street, 6th Floor
San Francisco, CA 94105-2445
415-744-6820

550 West "C" Street, Suite 550
San Diego, CA 92101
619-557-7250 ext. 1116

2719 North Air Fresno Drive
Fresno, CA 93727-1547
209-487-5791 ext. 106

660 J Street, Suite 215
Sacramento, CA 95814-1413
916-498-6410

200 West Santa Ana Blvd., Suite 700
Santa Ana, CA 92703-2352
714-550-7420 ext. 3711

330 N. Brand Blvd., Suite 1200
Glendale, CA 91203-4459
818-552-3304

301 East Stewart Street
Las Vegas, NV 89125-2527
702-388-6611

2828 North Central Ave., Suite 800
Phoenix, AZ 85004-1093
602-640-2293

238 Archbishop FC Flores Street
Agana, GU 96910-5188
671-472-7277
300 Ala Moana, Room 2314
P.O. Box 50207
Honolulu, HI 96850-4981
808-541-2990

REGION X
1200 6th Avenue, Suite 1700
Seattle, WA 98101-1128
206-553-7065

1515 SW Fifth Avenue, Suite 1050
Portland, OR 97201-5494
503-326-2682
Fax: 503-326-2808
e-mail: roger.wills@sba.gov

1020 Main Street, Suite 290
Boise, ID 83702-5745
208-334-9079

222 W. 8th Avenue #67, Room A36
Anchorage, AK 99513
907-271-4022

Appendix G

Minority Business Development Centers

Alabama
Birmingham MBDC
1718 Fifth Avenue, North
Birmingham, AL 35203
205-251-2040

Mobile MBDC
801 Executive Park Drive,
Suite 102
Mobile, AL 36606
205-471-5165

Alaska
Alaska MBDC
1577 C St., Plaza, Suite 304
Anchorage, AK 99501
907-274-5400

Arizona
Arizona NABDC
953 E. Juanita Avenue
Mesa, AZ 85204
602-831-7524

Phoenix MBDC
702 Osborne St., Suite 150
Phoenix, AZ 85014
602-225-0740

Tucson MBDC
1200 N. El Dorado Sq., Suite D-440
Tucson, AZ 85715
602-721-1187

American Indian Consultants, Inc.
2070 E. Southern Ave.
Tempe, AZ 85282
602-945-2635

California
Bakersfield MBDC
1706 Chester Ave., Suite 407
Bakersfield, CA 93301
805-633-2787

California NABDC
9650 Flair Drive, Suite 303
El Monte, CA 91731-3008
818-442-3701

Fresno MBDC
2300 Tulare St., Suite 210
Fresno, CA 93721
209-266-2766

Oxnard MBDC
741 S. A Street, Suite A
Oxnard, CA 93030
805-385-6277

Riverside MBDC
Vanir tower
290 N. D Street, Suite 303
San Bernadino, CA 92401
909-381-4008

Sacramento MBDC
1779 Tribute Road, Suite J
Sacramento, CA 95815
916-649-2551

Salinas MBDC
14 Maple Street, Suite D
Salinas, CA 93901
408-422-8825

San Diego MBDC
777 Alvarado Road, Suite 310
La Mesa, CA 91941
619-668-6232

San Francisco MBDC
221 Main Street, Suite 1350
San Francisco, CA 94105
415-243-8430

Oakland MBDC
1212 Broadway, Suite 900
Oakland, CA 94612
510-271-0180

San Jose MBDC
150 Almaden Blvd., Suite 600
San Jose, CA 95113
408-275-9456

Santa Barbara MBDC
331 N. Milpas Street, Suite G
Santa Barbara, CA 93103
805-965-2611

Colorado
Denver MBDC
930 W. 7th Avenue
Denver, CO 80204
303-623-5660

District of Columbia
Washington MBDC
1133 15th St., NW Suite 1120
Washington, DC 20005
202-785-2886

Florida
Miami/Ft.Lauderdale MBDC
1200 NW 78th Avenue, Suite 301
Miami, FL 33126
305-591-7355

Orlando MBDC
132 E. Colonial Drive, Suite 211
Orlando, FL 33126
407-422-6234

West Palm Beach MBDC
2001 Broadway, Suite 301
Riviera Beach, FL 33404
407-863-0895

Georgia
Atlanta MBDC
75 Piedmont Avenue, NE, Suite 256
Atlanta, GA 30303
404-586-0973

Augusta MBDC
1394 Laney-Walker Blvd.
Augusta, GA 30901-2796
706-722-0994

Columbus MBDC
233 12th Street, Suite 621
Columbus, GA 31920
706-324-4253

Hawaii
Honolulu MBDC
1132 Bishop Street, Suite 1000
Honolulu, HI 96813-3652
808-531-6232

Indiana
Gary MBDC
567 Broadway
P.O. Box 9007
Gary, IN 46402
219-883-5802

Indianapolis MBDC
4755 Kingsway Drive, Suite 103
Indianapolis, IN 46205
317-257-0327

Kentucky
Louisville MBDC
609 W. Main Street, 3rd Floor
Louisville, KY 40202
502-589-6232

Louisiana
Baton Rouge MBDC
2036 Wooddale Blvd., Suite D
Baton Rouge, LA 70806
504-924-0186

New Orleans MBDC
10001 Lake Forest Blvd., Suite 408
New Orleans, LA 70127
504-241-8664

Maryland
Baltimore MBDC
301 N. Charles St., Suite 902
Baltimore, MD 21201
410-752-7400

Michigan
Detroit MBDC
645 Griswold Street, Suite 2156
Detroit, MI 48226
313-963-6232

Minnesota
Minneapolis MBDC
2021 E. Hennepin Avenue,
Suite LL 35
Minneapolis, MN 55413
612-331-5576

Missouri
Kansas City MBDC
1101 Walnut Street, Suite 1900
Kansas City, MO 64106-2143
816-471-1520

St. Louis MBDC
231 S. Bemiston Street, Suite 750
St. Louis, MO 63105
314-721-7766

New Jersey
Middlesex/Somerset/Hunterdon
  MBDC
390 George Street, Suite 401
New Brnswick, NJ 08901
908-249-5511

New Mexico
Albuquerque MBDC
718 Central Ave. SW
Albuquerque, NM 87102
505-843-7114

Statewide New Mexico MBDC
718 Central SW
Albuquerque, NM 87102
505-843-7114

New York
Brooklyn MBDC
300 Flatbush Avenue, Suite 423
Brooklyn, NY 11217
718-522-5880

Buffalo MBDC
570 E. Delavan Ave.
Buffalo, NY 14211
716-895-2218

Manhattan MBDC
51 Madison Avenue, Suite 2212
New York, NY 10010
212-779-4364

Nassau/Suffolk MBDC
150 Broad Hollow Rd., Suite 304
Melville, NY 11747
516-549-5454

Queens MBDC
125-10 Queens Blvd., Suite 2705
Kew Gardens, NY 11415
718-793-3900

Rochester MBDC
350 North Street
Rochester, NY 14605
716-232-6120

Williamsburg/Brooklyn MBDC
12 Hayward Street
Brooklyn, NY 11211
718-522-5620

North Carolina
Charlotte MBDC
700 E. Stonewall Street, Suite 360
Charlotte, NC 28202
704-334-7522

Cherokee NABDC
Acquoni Building
Acquoni Road
P.O. Box 1200
Cherokee, NC 28719
704-497-9335

Cherokee NABDC
70 Woodfin Place, Suite 305
Asheville, NC 28801
704-252-2516

Fayetteville MBDC
114 ½ Anderson Street
Fayetteville, NC 28302
910-483-7513

Raleigh/Durham MBDC
817 New Bern Avenue, Suite 8
Raleigh, NC 27601
919-833-6122

North Dakota
North Dakota NABDC
3315 University Dr.
Bismarck, ND 58504-7596
701-255-6849

Ohio
Cincinnati MBDC
1821 Summit Road, Suite 111
Cincinnati, OH 45237-2810
512-679-6000

Cleveland MBDC
601 Lakeside, Suite 335
Cleveland, OH 44114
216-664-4155

Dayton MBDC
Society Bank Building
32 N. Main Street, Suite 903
Dayton, OH 45402
513-228-0290

Oklahoma
Oklahoma City MBDC
3017 N. MLK Ave.
Oklahoma City, OK 73111
405-424-0082

Tulsa MBDC
240 East Apache Street
Tulsa, OK 74106-3799
918-592-1995

Oregon
Portland MBDC
8959 SW Barbur Blvd., Suite 102
Portland, OR 97219
503-245-9253

Pennsylvania
Philadelphia MBDC
125 N. 8th Street 4th Floor
Philadelphia, PA 19106
215-569-3500

Pittsburgh MBDC
Nine Parkway Center, Suite 250
Pittsburgh, PA 15220
412-921-1155

Puerto Rico
Mayaguez MBDC
70 West Mendez Vigo
P.O. Box 3136 Marina Station
Mayaguez, PR 00681
809-833-7783

Ponce MBDC
Edificio El Pardo
19 Salud Street
Ponce, PR 00731
809-840-8100

San Juan MBDC
122 Eleanor Roosevelt Avenue
Hato Rey, PR 00919
809-753-8484

South Carolina
Charleston MBDC
4 Carriage Lane, Suite 201
Charleston, SC 29407
803-556-3040

Columbia MBDC
2111 Ball Street
Columbia, SC 29201
803-779-5905

Tennessee
Memphis MBDC
5 N. 3rd Street, Suite 301
Memphis, TN 38103
901-527-2298

Nashville MBDC
14 Academy Place, Suite 2
Nashville, TN 37210-2026
615-255-0432

Texas
Austin MBDC
1524 S. International Highway 35,
   Suite 218
Austin, TX 78704
512-447-0800

Beaumont MBDC
330 Liberty, 2nd Floor
Beaumont, TX 77701
409-835-0440

Brownsville MBDC
2100 Boca Chica Blvd., Suite 301
Brownsville, TX 78521-2265
512-546-3400

Corpus Christi MBDC
3649 Leopard Street, Suite 514
Corpus Christi, TX 78404
512-887-7961

Dallas/Ft. Worth MBDC
501 Wynnewood Village Shopping
   Center, Suite 202
Dallas, TX 75224-1899
214-943-4095

El Paso MBDC
6068 Gateway E., Suite 200
El Paso, TX 79905
915-774-0626

Houston MBDC
1200 Smith Street, Suite 2870
Houston, TX 77002
713-650-3831

McAllen MBDC
1701 W. Bus. Hwy. 83, Suite 306
McAllen, TX 78501
210-664-0073

San Antonio MBDC
1222 N. Main Street, Suite 750
San Antonio, TX 78212
210-558-2480

Utah
Salt Lake City MBDC
350 East 500 S., Suite 101
Salt Lake City, UT 84111
801-328-8181

Virginia
Hampton Roads MBDC
129 W. Virginia Beach, Suite 105
Hampton, VA 23510
804-626-1635

Richmond MBDC
3805 Cutshaw Avenue, Suite 402
Richmond, VA 23230
804-353-6227

Virgin Islands
Virgin Islands MBDC
31 Dronningens Gad
Drake's Passage, 2nd Floor
St. Thomas, VI 00802
809-777-4103

Washington
Northwest NABDC
100 W. Harrison
South Tower, Suite 530
Seattle, WA 98119
206-285-2190

Seattle MBDC
155 NE 100th Avenue, Suite 401
Seattle, WA 98105
206-525-5617

Wisconsin
Milwaukee MBDC
1442 N. Farwell Avenue, Suite 500
Milwaukee, WI 53202
414-289-3422

Appendix H

Mutual Fund Families

Aim	(800) 998-4246
Algers Fund	(800) 992-3863
Alliance	(800) 247-4154
American Funds	(800) 421-9900
American Skandia	(800) 752-6342
Ark Funds/SEI	(800) 275-3863
Banc Stock Group	(800) 226-5595
Baron	(800) 992-2766
Bear Stearns	(800) 766-4111
Blackrock Funds	(800) 227-7236
Calvert	(800) 368-2750
Chase Vista	(800) 348-4782
Cohen & Steers	(800) 437-9912
Conseco	(800) 888-4918
Countrywide Touchstone	(800) 669-2796
Davis Funds	(800) 279-2279
Delaware	(800) 362-7500
Dreyfus Premier Funds	(800) 334-6899
Eaton Vance	(800) 225-6265
Enterprise	(800) 432-4320
Evergreen	(800) 633-4900
Federated Funds	(800) 245-5051
Fidelity Advisors	(800) 526-0084
Fifth Investors	(800) 423-4026
Fifth Third Funds	(800) 654-5372
First American	(800) 814-3406

Flag Investors	(800) 767-3524
Forlis	(800) 800-2638
Forum Funds	(800) 943-6786
Franklin Templeton	(800) 342-5236
Gabelli Funds	(800) 422-3554
Galaxy Funds	(800) 628-0414
GAM	(800) 426-4685
Gateway Funds	(800) 354-6339
Goldman Sachs	(800) 762-5035
Govett Funds	(800) 634-6838
Guardian	(800) 221-3253
Hartford Funds	(800) 523-7798
Homestate Funds	(800) 232-0224
IDEX Funds	(800) 851-9777
ING/Pilgrim	(800) 334-3444
ISI Funds	(800) 955-7175
Ivy	(800) 456-5111
John Hancock	(800) 225-6020
Kemper	(800) 621-5027
Kensington Funds	(800) 253-2949
Lazard Funds	(800) 823-6300
Liberty	(800) 426-3750
Lord Abbett	(800) 426-1130
MainStay	(800) 624-6782
Mentor Funds/Evergreen	(800) 382-0016
MFS	(800) 343-2829
Montgomery Funds	(800) 572-3863
Monument Funds	(800) 527-9525
Munder	(800) 239-3334
Narragansett	(800) 453-6864
New Alternatives	(800) 423-8383
North American	(800) 872-8037
Nuveen-Flagship	(800) 351-4100
Ocean State	(800) 992-2207
Olstein	(800) 799-2113
One Group	(800) 480-4111
Oppenheimer	(800) 255-2755
Phoenix	(800) 255-2755
PIMCO Advisors	(800) 835-3401
Pioneer	(800) 225-6292
ProFunds	(888) 776-3637

Putnam	(800) 354-4000
RS Investments	(800) 766-3863
Seligman	(800) 221-2783
Sentinel Funds	(800) 282-3863
State Street Research	(800) 882-0052
SunAmerica	(800) 858-8850
Third Avenue Funds	(800) 443-1021
Thornberg	(800) 847-0200
Van Kampen	(800) 421-5666
VanEck	(800) 826-2333
Victory Funds	(800) 539-3863
Wells Fargo/Stagecoach	(800) 552-9612

NO-LOAD MUTUAL FUND COMPANIES

American Century	(800) 345-2021
Babson	(800) 422-2766
Benham	(800) 472-3389
Fidelity	(800) 544-8888
Founders	(800) 525-2440
Invesco	(800) 241-5477
Janus	(800) 525-3713
Kaufman	(800) 237-0132
Lexington	(800) 526-0056
Midas Funds (Bull & Bear)	(800) 400-6432
SAFECO	(800) 624-5711
Stein Roe	(800) 338-2550
T.Rowe Price	(800) 638-5660
United Services	(800) 873-8637
Value Line	(800) 223-0818
Vanguard	(800) 662-7447
Warburg Pincus	(800) 927-2874

Appendix I

Regional Securities and Exchange Commission Offices

SEC Headquarters
450 Fifth Street, NW
Washington, DC 20549
Office of Investor Education and
  Assistance
(202) 942-7040
e-mail: help@sec.gov

Northeast Regional Office
Securities and Exchange commission
Wayne M. Carlin, Regional Director
7 World Trade Center, Suite 1300
New York, NY 10048
(212) 748-8000
e-mail: new york@sec.gov

Boston District Office
Juan M. Marcelino, District
  Administrator
73 Tremont Street, Suite 600
Boston, MA 02108-3912
(617) 424-5900
e-mail: boston@sec.gov

Philadelphia District Office
Ronald C. Long, District
  Administrator
The Curtis Center, Suite 1120E
601 Walnut Street
Philadelphia, PA 19106-3322
(215) 597-3100
e-mail: philadelphia@sec.gov

Southeast Regional Office
David Nelson, Regional Director
1401 Brickell Avenue, Suite 200
Miami, FL 33131
(305) 536-4700
e-mail: miami@sec.gov

Atlanta District Office
Richard P. Wessel, District
  Administrator
3475 Lenox Road, N.E., Suite 1000
Atlanta, GA 30326-1232
(404) 842-7600
e-mail: atlanta@sec.gov

Midwest Regional Office
Mary Keefe, Regional Director
Citicorp Center, Suite 1400
500 W. Madison Street
Chicago, IL 60661-2511
(312) 353-7390
e-mail: chicago@sec.gov

Central Regional Office
Randall J. Fons, Regional Director
1801 California Street, Suite 4800
Denver, CO 80202-2648
(303) 844-1000
e-mail: denver@sec.gov

Fort Worth District Office
Harold F. Degenhardt, District
 Administrator
801 Cherry Street, 19th Floor
Fort Worth, TX 76102
(817) 978-3821
e-mail: dfw@sec.gov

Salt Lake District Office
Kenneth D. Israel, Jr., District
 Administrator
500 Key Bank Tower, Suite 500
50 South Main Street
Salt Lake City, UT 84144-0402
(801) 524-5796
e-mail: saltlake@sec.gov

Pacific Regional Office
Valerie Caproni, Regional Director
5670 Wilshire Boulevard, 11th Floor
Los Angeles, CA 90036-3648
(323) 965-3998
e-mail: losangeles@sec.gov

San Francisco District Office
Helane Morrison, District Admin.
44 Montgomery Street, Suite 1100
San Francisco, CA 94104
(415) 705-2500
e-mail: sanfrancisco@sec.gov

NOTE: A number of offices within
 the SEC can also be contacted via
 electronic mail.
 www.sec.gov/contact/addresses.htm

About the Author

A native of Boston, Melvin B. Miller has been actively involved in community public service for more than thirty years. In 1965, he founded the *Bay State Banner*, a weekly newspaper advocating the interests of Greater Boston's African-American community. Miller has served as the *Banner's* Publisher and Editor since its inception.

Prior to the establishment of the *Banner*, Melvin B. Miller was an Assistant U. S. Attorney for the District of Massachusetts. In 1973, the State Banking Commissioner appointed him as the Conservator of the Unity Bank and Trust Company, Boston's first minority bank.

Melvin B. Miller is also a founding partner of Fitch, Miller & Tourse, a primarily corporate law firm. He was also Vice President and General Counsel of WHDH-TV, Channel 7 in Boston.

A long-term trustee of Boston University, Melvin B. Miller is a member of the Executive Committee. He was also a Director of Project Step, a program to provide early training for talented minority violinists, cellists, and viola players. A member of the now disbanded National Advisory Council to American companies doing business in South Africa under the Sullivan Principles, he presently serves as a director of USSALEP (United States South Africa Leadership Exchange Program). Miller is a trustee of the Huntington Theatre Company, the Boston Medical Center, and Mass Inc., a public policy think tank. **He is also a director of the Boston Bank of Commerce.**

Melvin B. Miller is a graduate of Boston Latin School, Harvard University, and Columbia Law School.